SUEÑOS
WORLD SPANISH 1
ACTIVITY BOOK
NEW EDITION

Aurora Longo
and
Almudena Sánchez

BBC Active, an imprint of Educational Publishers LLP,
part of the Pearson Education Group
Edinburgh Gate, Harlow, Essex CM20 2JE, England

New edition published 2003

ISBN: 978-0-563-47247-6

The authors and publisher would like to thank the following for permission to
reproduce copyright material: Radio Nacional de España y el Instituto Cervantes
for an interview with Gloria Fuertes, page 19; *La Vanguardia*, Anuncios clasificados
26.2.95, page 21; *El País*, Boletín de suscripción 19.3.95, page 7; *El País*, anuncios
breves 16.2.95, page 21; *El País*, anuncios breves 22.4.93, page 22; *El País*, Roberto
Verino, Diseñador, "No despego los pies del suelo" 17.2.94, page 58; RENFE, page
31; Paradores de Turismo de España, page 36; *Revista Mía*, no. 433, "Los españoles
y el tiempo libre", page 55; Ronda Iberia de Iberia Líneas Aereas de España,
"Ferias: Expoarte" diciembre 1994, page 62; *Expansión*, "Los ingleses aprenden
español para hacer negocios" 10.11.93, page 68.

The publisher wishes to thank the owners of all copyright material reproduced
in this book. They regret that, although every attempt has been made to contact
all copyright owners concerned, this has not always been possible. They would be
glad to hear from any copyright owners with whom contact has not been made.

We are grateful to the following for their permission to reproduce copyright
material and photographs: Paradores de Turismo de España, page 36; *El País*
for weather illustrations, page 45; BBC Worldwide Ltd for pages 2 and 64; Rex
Features London for page 51; Tony Stone Worldwide/Raphael Koskas for page 64;
Richard Donnelly for page 64

Edited by Claire Thacker
Typesetting and design by Oxprint Design, Oxford
Illustrations by Oxford Illustrators, Oxford

Printed in Malaysia (CTP-VVP)

ARP Impression 98
Printed in Great Britain by Clays Ltd, St Ives plc

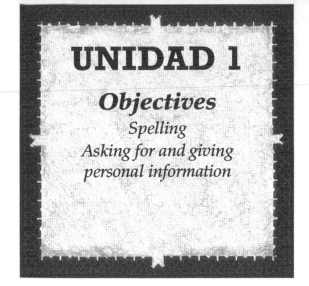

UNIDAD 1

Objectives
Spelling
Asking for and giving
personal information

1 El alfabeto

Spelling, pronunciation

a Can you say these letters in Spanish?

a c e g h i j k ñ q v w x y z

Check your answers on your recording, Unit 1 Track 3.

b You are speaking to a Spanish colleague on the phone. Spell the names of these clients.

John Clark   **Julia Gordon**   **Valery Wilson**
Javier Muñiz

2 Países y lenguas

SPELLING: *Countries and languages*

a There are some missing letters in these countries. Fill in the blanks with the correct letter.

AR _ _ NTINA   ALEMAN _ _

CH _ L _   HOLAND _

G _ _ _ BR _ TA _ A   PORTU _ _ _

J _ P _ N   ESPA _ A

b What languages are spoken in those countries?

Example: **En Argentina se habla español.**

3 Datos personales

Giving personal details about yourself

You are at a party and the hostess has introduced you to a Spanish friend of hers so that you can practise your Spanish. Answer Carlos's questions.

Carlos: **¿Cómo te llamas?**

Tú: Me llama es Dianne

Carlos: **¿Eres de Londres?**

Tú: No say de Grimsby.

Carlos: **¿Y dónde vives?**

Tú: Vivo en Lincolnshire

Carlos: **Oye, tu español es muy bueno. ¿Hablas otras lenguas?**

Tú: Si, me hablo alemaña

4 ¿Yo, tú, él/ella/usted?

Test your knowledge of Spanish verbs

You have seen the Spanish personal pronouns in the coursebook:

Yo, I; *tú*, you (informal); *él*, he; *ella*, she; *usted*, you (formal).

In Spanish you don't need to use these pronouns all the time since the verbs have different endings for each person. The trick is to recognise those endings.

se llama	eres	te llamas	habla
es	hablas	vivo	me llamo
hablo	vives	soy	vive

Yo	Tú	El/ella/usted
		se llama

5 *Ahora tú*

Asking for personal details in formal and informal situations

a Now it is your turn to ask your new Spanish friend questions at the party. Can you ask the right questions for these answers? Use the form *tú*, since the party is quite informal in this case.

¿ .... ? **Carlos.**

¿ .... ? **Soy de Sevilla.**

¿ .... ? **Vivo en Plymouth.**

¿ .... ? **Hablo español, claro, inglés y un poquito de francés.**

b What would your questions be in a more formal situation? Use the form *usted*.

Nombre: Beatriz
Lugar de origen: Rosario (Argentina)
Domicilio: Madrid (España)
Lenguas: español, francés

6 *Hablando de otros*

TALKING ABOUT OTHER PEOPLE:
Practice of the third person

Nombre: Pep
Lugar de origen: Barcelona (España)
Domicilio: Londres
Lenguas: español, catalán, inglés e italiano

Look at this text introducing one of these people:

Se llama Carlos. Es de Vigo, pero vive en Buenos Aires. Habla español e inglés.

Can you introduce the other two?

....

....

....

....

Nombre: Carlos
Lugar de origen: Vigo, (España)
Domicilio: Buenos Aires (Argentina)
Lenguas: español, inglés

7 Saludos y despedidas

Greetings

Look at the time and use the appropriate form of greeting.

Example: 9.00 Hola, buenos días.

8 ¿Me da su pasaporte?

Reading for specific information

PASAPORTE Nº/PASSPORT Nº

Apellidos: Gómez Martínez

Nombre: Marta

Nacionalidad: española   Sexo: Mujer

Fecha de nacimiento: 10.4.1956   Oficina expedidora: Sans 28

Lugar de nacimiento: Montevideo (Uruguay)

Domicilio: Paseo de Gracia 110, Barcelona

Firma del titular:

M. Gómez Martínez

M. Gómez Martínez

Fecha de expedición 30.6.94

Fecha de caducidad 30.6.2004

P(ESP(Z458985(RES 9002722(1259160((((((((((<<

Look at this passport and answer the following questions.

1 What is the full name of this person?

2 What is her nationality?

3 When and where was she born?

4 Where does she live?

5 For how long is the passport valid?

9 Es muy fácil. (It's very easy!)

There are quite a few words that are very similar both in Spanish and English. Look at the illustrations and try to make up the Spanish words with the letters provided.

a arb   d asparopet   g puroeraeto

b teloh   e éfnoloet

c spaltoih   f autsreanret

10 ¿Qué sabes en español? (What do you already know in Spanish?)

Testing your vocabulary

There are many Spanish words which are internationally known. How many do you know? Write them in the columns below.

Names	Food and drink	Others

UNIDAD 2

Objectives

*Asking for and giving
personal details
Introducing people
Describing your family*

1 Vocabulario

Testing your vocabulary

a Look at these groups of words and spot the
odd-one-out.

Example: **1 médico – it is not a nationality**

1 inglés francés (médico) canadiense
2 arquitecto padre hija tío
3 pintor actor profesor alemana
4 italiana hermana española mexicana
5 secretaria madre abuela marido
6 estudiante enfermera carpintero marido

b Classify the words above into these three
groups:

Nacionalidad	Profesión	Familia

2 En una conferencia

*Introducing people. Giving personal details
about others*

a At an international conference some
speakers are being introduced to the
audience. Look at the business card (*tarjeta
de visita*) and complete the text with these
words:

es	es	vive	esta	trabaja

CARMEN HERRERA
Arquitecta

Proyectisa Internacional, S.A
C/ Fortuny 32
28010 Madrid

..... es Carmen Herrera. ..... española y .....
en Madrid.
..... arquitecta y ..... en la empresa Proyectisa
Internacional.

b Introduce these people to the participants.

Costa Rica

Rodolfo Prados
Ingeniero

Construcciones S.A.
C/Ramos
San José

....
....

Francia

Nicole Dubois
Profesora

Universidad de Nantes
Rue Michelot
44000 Nantes

....
....

Portugal

Rosa Oliveira
Diseñadora

Ofimagen, S.L. Rua Dourador Lisboa

....
....

Italia

Roberto Manzoni
Pintor

Escuela de Arte de Milán
Via Castello
Milán

....
....

c Now introduce yourself to the audience.

....
....

3 *En el descanso*

a In the break at the conference more introductions are necessary.

Complete the dialogues using the appropriate register: *tú* or *usted*.

1 A: **Señor Orson.** ..... **presento** .... **señora Ortega, de Colombia.**

B: .....

A: **Encantada.**

2 A: **Mira, John.** ..... **presento** ..... **Ingrid.**

B: **Hola, ¿qué tal?**

C: .....

b Introduce these other people.

1 Señor Lobos, España/ Señora Losada, Argentina

....
....

2 Sergio, Colombia/ Roberto, Ecuador

....
....

3 Señora Arribas, Costa Rica/ Señor Peña, Venezuela

....
....

4 Carlos, Bolivia/Luisa, Honduras

....
....

4 Gente nueva

Practising your dialogue skills

Carla and Javier have just met and they are exchanging some personal details about themselves. Complete the dialogue with the information in the boxes.

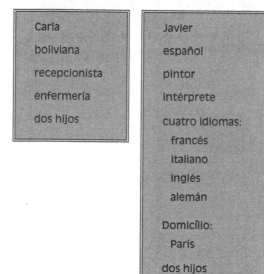

Carla	Javier
boliviana	español
recepcionista	pintor
enfermería	intérprete
dos hijos	cuatro idiomas:
	francés
	italiano
	inglés
	alemán
	Domicîlio:
	París
	dos hijos

Javier: Carla, tú no eres española, ¿verdad?

Carla: No, ...

Javier: ¿Y a qué te dedicas?

Carla: .... pero
.... Es mi
vocación. ¿Y tú en
.... ?

Javier: Soy .... pero
....

Carla: ¿Sí? ¿ .... ?

Javier: Cuatro: inglés, francés, italiano, alemán.
Y español, claro.

Carla: ¿ .... ?

Javier: En París, con mi mujer y mis hijos.

Carla: ¿ .... ?

Javier: Dos, un niño y una niña.

Carla: Yo .... tengo dos
hijos ...

5 En la recepción del hotel

Giving personal details about yourself

You have just arrived at your hotel and the receptionist is asking you some questions. Answer her questions.

¿Cómo se llama?

....

¿Cuál es su nacionalidad?

....

¿Y su dirección?

....

¿A qué se dedica?

....

¿Y su lugar de trabajo?

....

¿Tiene teléfono?

....

Muchas gracias. Aquí tiene su llave.

....

6 La familia

a This is Beatriz's family. Can you say who is who?

Example: **Arturo es su hermano.**

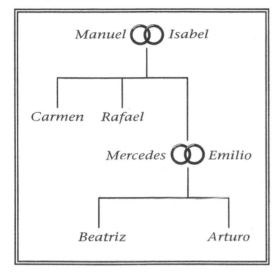

1 **Rafael es** ....

2 **Emilio es** ....

3 **Mercedes es** ....

4 **Carmen es** ....

5 **Manuel e Isabel son** ....

b Beatriz introduces some members of her family to a friend, Lola, who is visiting her. Complete the dialogues with words from the box.

ésta	es	mi	éste

1 *Beatriz:* **Lola, ... madre.**

   Lola: **Encantada.**

   Mercedes: **Encantada.**

2 *Beatriz:* **..... .... padre.**

   Lola: **Encantada.**

   Emilio: **Encantado.**

3 *Beatriz:* **Y .... hermano Arturo.**

   Lola: **Hola.**

   Arturo: **Hola.**

7 Una suscripción

You want to receive *El País* every day at home. Fill in the form with your personal details.

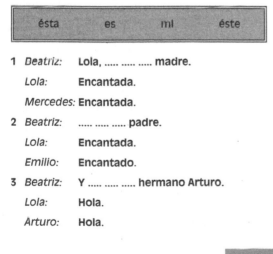

Este País llegará muy lejos

Cada semana, las noticias más importantes de EL PAIS llegarán donde desee: EE.UU., Japón, Inglaterra, Brasil, Suecia … a cualquier lugar del mundo.

EL PAIS
EDICIÓN INTERNACIONAL
EL PANORAMA MÁS COMPLETO DE LA INFORMACIÓN SEMANAL

SUSCRÍBASE O REGALE UNA SUSCRIPCIÓN

Suscripción a EL PAIS, Edición Internacional (marque con una ✗ lo que le interese) por un periodo de:

DOMINGOS	☐ 3 MESES EUR	☐ 6 MESES EUR	☐ 1 AÑO EUR
Extranjero (c normal).....................	62,00	111,00	216,00
Europa y norte de África (c aéreo)....	92,00	171,00	330,00
América (c aéreo)	140,00	267,00	487,00
Asia Oriental y Oceanía (c aéreo)...	200,00	382,00	727,00

ENVIAR A:

NOMBRE Y APELLIDOS

TELÉFONO

DIRECCIÓN

CIUDAD   C POSTAL

PROVINCIA, DEPARTAMENTO O ESTADO

PAIS

Formas de pago: En dólares USA, o su contravalor en cualquier otra moneda convertible, a DIARIO EL PAÍS, S. A.

☐ Domiciliación bancaria

Banco/Caja   Nº Agencia

Dirección   Población

Provincia   No c/c

☐ Tarjeta de crédito

☐ American Express ☐ Visa ☐ Diners ☐ Master ☐ Cajamadrid y Red 6000

Nº de tarjeta

Fecha de caducidad

FIRMA DEL TITULAR

Envíe este boletín a DIARIO EL PAÍS, S. A. Departamento de Suscripciones. C/Miguel Yuste, 40. 28037 Madrid (España) Teléfono 91 337 82 69. Fax 91 337 83 87

UNIDAD 3

Objectives

Recognising adjective endings
Asking where public places are
Describing places

1 El pueblo y la ciudad

Recognising feminine and masculine endings

The words in the box below are adjectives used to describe what a place is like. As you know Spanish nouns can be feminine or masculine and the adjectives change their endings according to the gender. Look at the endings of the adjectives in the box and then match them with *un pueblo* or *una ciudad*.

pequeño	turística	aburrido
antiguo	acogedor	ruidosa
tranquilo	bonita	alegre
moderna	acogedora	grande

Un pueblo	Una ciudad

2 Descripciones

Practising the form of adjectives describing places

Match the adjectives on the left with their opposites on the right.

1	moderna	a	moderno
2	grandes	b	pequeños
3	bonitos	c	divertidas
4	aburridas	d	bonita
5	modernos	e	antigua
6	fea	f	feos
7	antiguo	g	antiguos

3 Sopa de letras (Word search)

Testing your vocabulary of public places

a There are ten public places hidden in the word search (*sopa de letras*). Can you find them?

S	T	E	A	T	R	O	H	I	R	J	K
B	A	I	I	P	A	R	Q	U	E	Z	Q
N	W	S	G	A	P	T	Y	L	S	R	A
E	C	H	L	P	E	N	M	A	T	V	R
S	U	P	E	R	M	E	R	C	A	D	O
T	Z	O	S	S	I	U	D	P	U	N	S
A	S	P	I	N	O	B	K	E	R	A	B
N	G	F	A	R	M	A	C	I	A	T	A
C	L	I	S	P	N	R	V	O	N	O	N
O	A	R	E	N	A	N	L	I	T	O	C
A	T	H	O	T	E	L	K	U	E	A	O

b ¿*Un* or *una*? Decide whether the words you found in a) are feminine or masculine and add *un* or *una*.

Example: **un mercado**

c El plural. Now transform the words into their plural form.

Example: **un mercado – unos mercados**

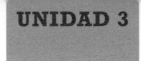
4 Un poco de orden, por favor

Word order

a Julian is staying in a Spanish town. He is making some enquiries about where certain places are but the word order in his sentences is not quite right. Can you help him by putting the words in the correct order?

1 ¿aquí hay estanco por un?

.... ☐

2 ¿de cerca aquí farmacia una hay?

.... ☐

3 ¿si decir puede me un hotel por hay aquí?

.... ☐

b These are the answers to Julian's questions. Match each question with the appropriate answer.

a) Sí, hay una en la Calle Mayor.

b) Sí, el Ritz, en la Avenida de Extremadura.

c) Sí, en la Plaza de la Constitución hay uno.

5 ¿Hay un ...?

You are in a Spanish town and you need to buy these things. Ask where the appropriate shops are.

1 ¿Hay un estanco por aquí?

2 ....

3 ....

4 ....

5 ....

6 ....

7 ....

6 En el hotel

Practising your dialogue skills: giving information about where places are

The manager of the Hotel Continental is helping some of the hotel customers to find their way around town. Look at the map and imagine what the manager's answers would be.

Example: ¿Hay un banco por aquí?
Sí, hay uno en el Paseo de Moratín y otro en la Plaza de las Carmelitas.

a) ¿Hay una tienda de ropa por aquí?

....

b) ¿Me puede decir si hay un museo cerca?

....

c) ¿Hay un estanco cerca de aquí?

....

d) ¿Hay una iglesia por aquí cerca?

....

e) ¿Hay restaurantes típicos cerca del hotel?

....

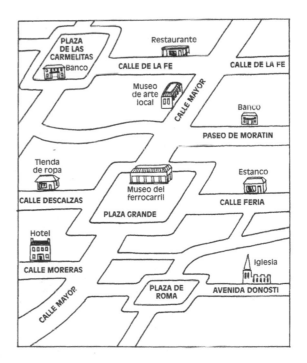

7 El barrio

Describing places: testing your overall vocabulary

Look at the picture and complete the text with the words in the box.

muchos	hay	en
de	varias	bares
antigua	cerca	muy
tranquilo	el	una
pero	un	

El barrio de Vistalegre es pequeño y ..... En la Calle Ronda ..... un supermercado y ..... tiendas de comestibles y ropa. Cerca del supermercado, ... la calle Casino, hay dos ..... y ..... iglesia. No ..... grande pero interesante y ..... En ..... Paseo de Miraflores hay ..... estanco y una Oficina ..... Correos. No hay ..... lugares de entretenimiento, ... hay un cine ..... del parque.

8 Un poco de turismo

Practising your reading skills

Read the text and answer these questions.

1 ¿Cómo se llama la ciudad? ....
2 ¿Qué monumentos hay? ....
3 ¿Cuál de esos monumentos tiene una longitud de casi un kilómetro? ....
4 ¿Qué otras cosas ofrece la ciudad?
....

UN PUENTE COMO UN ACUEDUCTO.

ven

Visita Segovia, Ciudad Patrimonio de la Humanidad.

Este fin de semana cógete un puente como un Acueducto. Ven a Segovia. Descubrirás una de las obras más grandiosas del imperio romano, con casi un kilómetro de longitud y ciento sesenta y siete arcos: El Acueducto. Podrás conquistar la ciudad desde su Alcázar amurallado y en la Plaza Mayor una Catedral, que es una obra de arte. Además, el placer del buen comer y beber, la artesanía, el folclore y el tipismo se dan cita en cada esquina. Por algo Segovia posee el título de Ciudad Patrimonio de la Humanidad.

Ven a Castilla y León.
¡Y lo tendrás todo!

Junta de Castilla y León

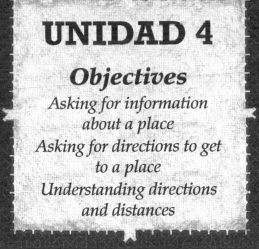

UNIDAD 4

Objectives

Asking for information about a place
Asking for directions to get to a place
Understanding directions and distances

1 ¿Dónde está ...?

Asking for and giving information

Complete the dialogue with the information on the map.

A: **Perdona, ¿ .... estanco por aquí?**

B: **Sí, hay uno .... Justicia,**
.... y la farmacia.

A: **¿Y puede .... dónde ....**
el mercado?

B: **En la ...., ...**
la lavandería.

A: **¿ .... un restaurante barato?**

B: **............................... Ronda, a la ....,**
.... del bar.

A: **Por último, ¿dónde .... coger el**
autobús 29? Necesito ir al centro.

B: **Pues, ... del bar, en la misma calle**
Ronda.

A: **Muchas gracias.**

B: **De nada.**

2

In all these sentences there is a missing word. Can you say which one and where?

Example: **Hay una farmacia enfrente del restaurante.**

1 **Hay bar enfrente del restaurante.**
2 **La farmacia enfrente del hospital.**
3 **Hay una parada de autobús delante bar.**
4 **Mi casa está la izquierda.**
5 **Museo arqueológico está en la calle Serrano.**
6 **¿Me da un horario autobuses?**
7 **Toledo está 72 km. de Madrid.**

3 Números

Practising numbers

Read these numbers and write the reverse number.

Example: **treinta y nueve (39) – noventa y tres (93)**

1 **veinticinco** ....
2 **sesenta y siete** ....
3 **ochenta y seis** ....
4 **catorce** ....
5 **noventa y ocho** ....
6 **cincuenta y seis** ....

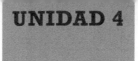

4 *Practising ordinal numbers*

How would you answer these questions? Look at the information and then try and answer them.

1 ¿Quién es María?

1° 2° 3^a 4°

....

2 ¿En qué piso vives?

1°, puerta 3^a

....

3 ¿La calle Mayor, por favor?

....

4 ¿La oficina del Sr. López?

5^a

2°

....

5 ¿Y la oficina del Sr. Pérez?

4^a

3°

....

6 ¿Quién es Pepe?

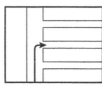

1° 2°

....

5 *En la oficina de turismo*

Asking for places and directions

You are in a tourist office in Spain and need some information. Can you ask the questions?

A: ¿ .... un plano de la ciudad?

B: Lo siento mucho, pero no tenemos ninguno.

A: ¡ Qué mala suerte! ¿ .... cómo .... al Museo de la Marina?

B: Sí, cómo no. Sigues recto hasta el .... de esta calle y coges la segunda a la derecha.

A: ¿ .... ?

B: No, está muy cerca.

A: ¿Y .... restaurante típico cerca del museo?

B: Sí, enfrente del Museo está el Bodegón.

A: ¿ .... ?

B: Pues sí, es un poquito caro, pero muy bueno.

A: Vale, muchas gracias.

6 *¿En qué dirección?*

Giving directions

Match the illustrations with the sentences.

a giras a la derecha

b sigues todo recto

c tomas la segunda a la izquierda

d cruzas la plaza

e sigues hasta el final de la calle

f giras a la izquierda

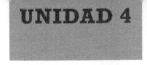
7 La princesa y el tesoro

Giving directions

a Can you help the prince to rescue his sweetheart? Write the directions he should follow.

Example: **Sigues todo recto, coges la primera a la izquierda y** ....
....

b Now she is free, but they need some money for their honeymoon. Help them to reach the treasure (*tesoro*).

....
....
....
....

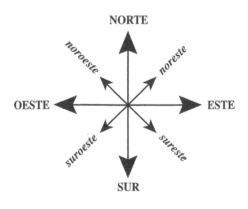

8 Un poco de geografía

Practising your reading and writing skills.

a Read the texts and locate the Spanish towns on the map.

1 Cádiz es una hermosa ciudad situada en la costa atlántica, en el suroeste de España. En ella pueden encontrarse enormes casas de estilo colonial rodeadas de palmeras.

2 Con un clima húmedo muy similar al clima de Gran Bretaña, A Coruña es una delicia para el visitante. Está en el noroeste español muy cerca de Santiago de Compostela. Sus playas son grandes y agradables y la gastronomía regional es excelente por la frescura de sus ingredientes y la gracia de su preparación.

3 Zaragoza es famosa por la amabilidad y jovialidad de sus gentes. Situada en el interior de la península, a unos 300 km de Barcelona, tiene un clima muy extremo, con temperaturas muy altas en verano y muy frías en invierno. La Basílica del Pilar es centro de grandes celebraciones y peregrinajes. El Barrio del Tubo es famoso por sus bares y sus excelentes tapas.

b Write similar paragraphs about these Guatemala towns using the information provided.

UNIDAD 5

Objectives

Buying food
Asking for an item
Asking for prices
Asking for quantities

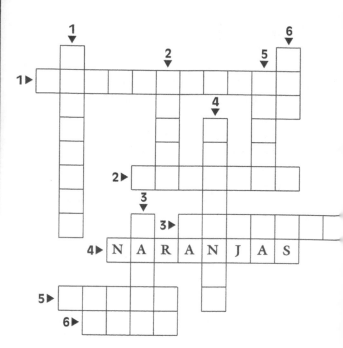

1 Alimentos

a Test your vocabulary with a game!
Complete the crossword using the drawings
as clues.

▶ ACROSS

1

2

3

4

5

6

▼ DOWN

1

2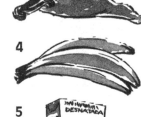

3

4

5

6

b Complete the box below with the products
from Activity 1a.

una botella de	vino
un litro de	
una barra de	
una bolsa de	
un paquete de (3 possibilities)	
un trozo de (×2)	
un kilo de (×2)	

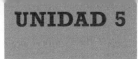

2 Las tiendas

Revising your vocabulary

Fill in the missing letters to find the names of shop types.

1 Pe_cadería

2 Fru__ría

3 Pa__dería

4 Char_utería

5 C_nfitería

Now reorder the missing letters to make the name of another shop.

_ _ _ _ _ _ _

3 En el supermercado

Vocabulary: food and drinks

a You are in the local supermarket (*supermercado*). Which counter will you go to to find the following food and drinks? Use your dictionary if necessary.

cerveza judías verdes pollo sardinas
vino cebollas ron truchas calamares
chuletas de cerdo conejo atún gambas
chorizo salchichón mangos aguacates
lechuga tomates queso manchego
manzanas cava tequila

Example: bebidas – cava

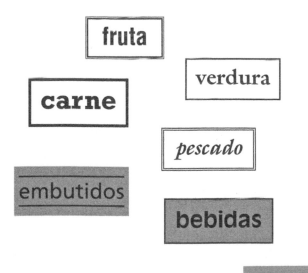

b Now make your own shopping list with the items available at the counters. Don't forget to specify the amounts you need.

b Now make your own shopping list with the items available at the counters. Don't forget to specify the amounts you need.

4 ¿Cuánto, cuántos, cuántas?

Use of quantifiers

Complete the following sentences using *Cuánto, Cuántos, Cuántas.*

Example: ¿Cuántos aguacates quiere?

1 ¿ .... manzanas quiere?

2 ¿ .... mangos quiere?

3 ¿ .... lechugas quiere?

4 ¿ .... es?

5 ¿ .... botellas de vino quiere?

5 Más números

Practising your numbers

Match the words with the numbers and then write the missing words.

567	780	1.879	135	2.500
100	5.768	6.690	14.975	458

cien

cuatrocientos cincuenta y ocho

mil ochocientos setenta y nueve

....

....

....

....

....

....

....

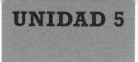

6 Preparando el aperitivo

Practising your dialogue skills

Some friends are coming to your house tonight and you want to offer them some snacks and some drinks. You need to do some shopping. Here is your shopping list. You are in the shop and want to buy what is on your list.

Complete the following dialogue.

Dependiente: **Buenos días.**

Tú: . ...

Dependiente: **¿Qué desea?**

Tú: ....

Dependiente: **Este de Rioja es buenísimo.**
              ¿Algo más?

Tú: **Sí, ... de queso.**

Dependiente: **Aquí tiene. ¿Quiere algo más?**

Tú: **¿ .... ?**

Dependiente: **¿Serrano o de York?**

Tú: **Serrano. ....**

Tú: **Ah, quería también ....**

Dependiente: **Aquí tiene. ¿Algo más?**

Tú: ....

        ¿ .... ?

Dependiente: **Son 15,32 euros.**

Shopping list (handwritten):

- 1 botella de vino tinto
- ½ kg. de queso
- ¾ de jamón serrano
- 1 bolsa de patatas grande

7 Platos típicos

Read the following recipe ingredients and match them with the appropriate name of the dish.

1 **Arroz a la cubana**

2 **Guacamole**

3 **Gazpacho**

a Ingredientes:
4 tomates maduros; 1/2 cebolla; 2 chiles verdes; 1 lima o 1 limón; 1 aguacate; sal y pimienta

b Ingredientes:
1 kg. de tomates pelados; 1/2 cebolla, 1 pepino, 1/4 kg. miga de pan (del día anterior y remojada en agua), sal, 1 taza de aceite de oliva, 2 cucharadas de vinagre, agua

c Ingredientes:
1/2 kg. de arroz; agua hirviendo abundante; 6 huevos, 1/4 litro de aceite; 6 plátanos medianos

24

UNIDAD 6

Objectives

Describing your daily routine

Saying how often you do things

1 Daily routines

Revising your vocabulary

a Add the vowels and you will find the infinitive of ten verbs related to daily routines.

Example: t r _ b _ j _ r – **trabajar**

1 d _ s _ y _ n _ r   6 _ m p _ z _ r

2 t _ r m _ n _ r   7 _ c _ s t _ r s _

3 c _ m _ r   8 _ r

4 s _ l _ r   9 c _ n _ r

5 v _ l v _ r   10 l _ v _ n t _ r s _

b Use the infinitives you found in Activity 1a and complete the text below.

Example: **Marisa es profesora, trabaja en la Universidad.**

Marisa es profesora, ... en la Universidad. Los días de trabajo .... a las siete. Todos los días .... café y tostadas. .... de casa a las ocho. .... a trabajar en metro. .... a trabajar a las nueve. A las dos .... al bar con sus compañeros. Normalmente .... un sandwich y una ensalada y a veces una pizza. Marisa .... de trabajar a las seis y .... a su casa sobre las siete. Prepara la cena y .... a las nueve y media. Normalmente .... a las doce.

c Write a paragraph about your own daily routine using all these verbs.

2 Entrevista

Read the text about Marisa again. Imagine you have to interview her about her daily routine. What questions do you think you would ask her?

Example: **¿A qué hora te levantas?**
Me levanto a las siete.

1 ¿ .... ?
   Café y tostadas.

2 ¿ .... ?
   A las nueve.

3 ¿ .... ?
   En metro.

4 ¿ .... ?
   Con mis compañeros.

5 ¿ .... ?
   A las siete.

6 ¿ .... ?
   A las doce.

3 A, de, en, por

Practising prepositions

In the following sentences there is a preposition missing. Can you write them down?

Example: ¿Desayunas casa?
¿Desayunas en casa?

1 *¿A que hora vuelves casa normalmente?*

2 *¿Trabajas la tarde?*

3 *¿Vas a trabajar autobús?*

4 *¿A qué hora terminas trabajar?*

5 *Normalmente salgo casa muy temprano.*

6 *¿A qué hora empiezas trabajar?*

7 *¿Trabajas una oficina?*

8 *¿qué hora os acostáis?*

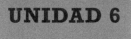

4 *El fin de semana*

Practising the verbs

In this dialogue two colleagues are talking about what they do during the weekend. Read the dialogue and fill in the gaps with the correct form of the verbs in brackets.

Example: **Ana y yo nos levantamos tarde.**

Juan: **¿Qué hacéis normalmente los sábados?**

Pedro: **Ana y yo (levantarse) ....
tarde, (desayunar) .... y (leer)
.... el periódico. Después
(limpiar) .... la casa un poco y
(hacer) .... la compra en el
supermercado. Antes de comer, (tomar)
.... un aperitivo cerca de casa con los
amigos del barrio. Por la noche,
(salir) .... siempre, (ir) ....
al cine, al teatro y luego a tomar una
cerveza.**

Juan: **Pues nosotros, todos los sábados (ir)
.... al gimnasio y luego (comer)
.... en casa de los padres de
Elena. Por la tarde, casi siempre nos
quedamos en casa, (escuchar)
.... música o (leer) ....
Normalmente (acostarse) ....
pronto porque todos los domingos
(ir) .... al campo. Ya sabes, que tenemos
una casa en el Escorial ...**

5 *¿Cuántas veces ...?*

Practising expressions of frequency

Paco and Marta are a couple who have a lodger, Antonio, who shares their flat and the household chores. The chart below shows the duty rota.

a Complete the chart with your own information.

	Antonio	*Paco y Marta*	*Tú*
Barrer	Lu & Mi	Ma & Vi & Do	
Fregar los platos	Do & Lu & Ma	Ma & Vi & Do	
Lavar la ropa		Ju & Sa	
Planchar	Do	Mi & Sa	
Sacar la basura	Lu & Vi	Ma & Mi Ju & Do	
Preparar la cena		Lu & Ma & Mi & Ju Vi & Sa & Do	

b Now write sentences about the people in the chart, using time expressions when appropriate.

Example: **Antonio barre a veces/ los lunes y miércoles / dos días a la semana.**
Paco y Marta barren tres veces a la semana.
(Yo) barro ...

6 Reading: Daily routines

a Gloria Fuertes was a well known person in Spain. The text opposite is a transcript of a radio programme in which she explained her daily routine. Read the text and guess what Gloria Fuertes's job was.

b Read the text again and mark the following statements True or False.

1 **Se levanta tarde.** *True*
2 **Se ducha antes de desayunar.**
3 **Nunca lee el periódico.**
4 **Se toma un güisqui despues de desayunar.**
5 **Ve la televisión después de comer.**
6 **Nunca duerme la siesta.**

Gloria Fuertes: Me acuesto tarde, por tanto, me levanto tarde. Lo primero que hago es hacerme un café. Vivo sola. Me tomo el café, con leche. Segunda cosa: ducha. Tercera cosa: leer el periódico. Me interesa lo que pasa en el mundo. Después de leer el periódico, no sé qué hacer: si tomar una aspirina o un güisqui. Escribo, dejo el periódico y escribo. Siempre tengo que escribir algo: o un poema o un cuento. A las tres, como. Veo un rato la tele: las noticias o algún programa. Descanso. Lo mejor de España, entre muchas cosas, es la siesta. Yo la practico. Una horita de siesta. Y luego, a leer y a escribir. A veces salgo a alguna exposición o a ver amigos. Pero cualquier día es a base de leer, escribir y soledad.

UNIDAD 7

Objectives

Understanding addresses
Describing types of houses and facilities
Describing your house
Expressing likes and dislikes

1 *La dirección*

Understanding addresses

a Can you match the abbreviation on the left with the appropriate word on the right?

1	P°	a	Calle
2	Pza.	b	Paseo
3	C/	c	Avenida
4	Avda.	d	esquina
5	esq.	e	Plaza
6	n°	f	número

b You are sending a letter to some friends but the addresses seem to be mixed up. Can you sort out the details and write them on the envelopes? You also need to use the right abbreviation.

1 Paseo del Prado
Beatriz Sierra
número 59, 7° B
28002 Madrid

2 Jose Luis Porta
La Habana
Cuba
Calle 29 esquina a la Plaza de San Rafael

3 Ciudad de Guatemala
32 Avenida 27-22, Zona 5
Francisco Mendoza
Guatemala

2 Los anuncios

Understanding advertisements

You are interested in the housing market in
Madrid and have decided to look in the
advertisement section in the newspaper.

a Under which numbers do you need to look
if you want to:

– alquilar un piso
– alquilar un apartamento
– alquilar un chalé en la playa para el verano

b Can you look through these adverts and
find the abbreviations for:

1 habitación ....
2 ascensor ....
3 calefacción ....
4 terraza ....
5 cocina nueva ....
6 cocina equipada ....
7 puerta blindada (*reinforced door*) ....

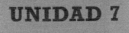

EL PAÍS, jueves 13 de febrero de 2003

ANUNCIOS BREVES

EDICIÓN NACIONAL: ANUNCIO NORMAL, 2.65 € LA PALABRA;
DOMINGO, 3.85 € DESTACADO, 4.10 € LA PALABRA;
DOMINGO, 6 €, MÍNIMO ADMITIDO, TRES PALABRAS

INMOBILIARIA VENTAS

101. Pisos
102. Apartamentos
103. Chalés
104. Locales comerciales
105. Oficinas
106. Rústicas
107. Terrenos/Solares
108. Plazos de garaje
109. Otros

INMOBILIARIA ALQUILER

201. Pisos (ofertas)
202. Pisos (demandas)
203. Chalés (ofertas)
204. Chalés (demandas)
205. Apartamentos (ofertas)
206. Apartamentos (demandas)
207. Locales/oficinas (ofertas)
208. Locales/oficinas (demandas)
209. Solares (ofertas)
210. Solares (demandas)
211. Hospedaje (ofertas)
212. Hospedaje (demandas)
213. Habitaciones (ofertas)
214. Habitaciones (demandas)
215. Plazas de garaje (ofertas)
216. Plazas de garaje (demandas)
217. Otros

INMOBILIARIA COMPRAS

301. Pisos
302. Apartamentos
303. Chalés

304. Locales comerciales
305. Oficinas
306. Rústicas
307. Terrenos/Solares
308. Otros

SERVICIOS INMOBILIARIOS

351. Traspasos
352. Hipotecas/créditos
353. Construcción
354. Pintura
355. Decoración
356. Electricidad
357. Cristalería
358. Cerrajería
359. Carpintería
360. Carpintería de aluminio
361. Jardinería
362. Albañilería y reformas
363. Mudanzas
364. Limpieza y mantenimiento
365. Otros

VACIONES

PLAYA
401. Ventas
402. Alquileres
403. Compras
SIERRA
411. Ventas
412. Alquileres
413. Compras
INTERIOR
421. Varios

12

CLASIFICADOS

sasi

JT.P.FABRA I PUIG.
T/exterior. 3 hab., baño, salón, cocina, galeria, tza., carpinter, aluminio, ascen. 119.000.€ F.412–41–41.
MARAGALL-AMILCAR.
L. vivir, 3 h., baño, aseo, salón, cocina nva., galeria, pta. bli., suelo ceram., ptas. emb., carp. alumin., asc. 163.900 €. F.412–41–41.
SANT DALMIR-M. COLL
Sobreático. Magnificas vistas. Todo exterior, 2 hab., aseo, salón, coc., galeria, 2 terrazas. 108.000 €. F.412–41–41.
MORATIN-ROCAFULL.
M. posibilidades, 3 hab., aseo, salón, coc., galeria. 84.000 €. F.412–41–41.
AMILCAR-CARTELLA
Atico, 2 h, aseo, salón, cocina, galeria, terraza, carp.-alumin., altillo, ascen. 99.000 €. F.412–41–41.
FENALS-V. FAVENCIA.
T/exterior, 3 hab., baño, salón, cocina, galeria, pta. blindada, ptas. emb., carp-alum., suelo ceramic. 79.900 €. F.412–41–41.

Así de fácil.

ANDREU-AGUSTIMILA.
Listo vivir, 3 hab, baño nvo., salón, cocina nva., galeria, tza., calef., ptas. emb., carp. alum , ascens. 159.000 €. F.412–41–41.
CASAS I AMIGO.
Impecable, 3 hab., baño nvo., salón, cocina nva., galeria, tza., bli., ptas. emb., asc., zona ajardinad. 158.500 €. F.412–41–41.
MALGRAT-FAB.I PUIG.
Casa con piscina, 3 hab., baño, salón, coc. equip., ptas. emb., carp. aluminio, 2 terrazas, trastero, ilar foc. jardín, sol todo el día 314.900 €. F.412–41–41.
RIERAD'HORTA.
Impecable, 4 hab., baño, salón, coc. equip., calef., pta. bli., carpinte. pvc., ptas. emb., parquet, park, opc., ascensor, zona infantil. 226.500 €. F.412–41–41.
FLORIDA-R. DE JANEIRO
Atico, gran terraza, 2 hab., baño, salón comedor, pta. blind., carpinter aluminio. 128.000 €. F.412–41–41.

LA VANGUARDIA **15**

sasi

JORD.S.JORDI-FELIPII.
Casa grdes tzas., 4 hab., baño, aseo, salón, cocina off., calef., pta. blind., parquet. 259.000 €. F.412–41–41.
JT.VIA LAIETANA
Impecable, 2 hab., baño, salón, cocina office, puerta. blind., suel. gres, trastero, carpint. aluminio 119.900 €. F.412–41–41.
S. ELM.-AL.CERVERA.
Listo vivir. 2 hab., aseo, salón, coc., pta. bl., altillo. 49.900 €. F.412–41–41.
P.JOAN DE BORBO.
Listo para vivir, 4 hab., baño, salón, cocina equip., cerram. madera, vistas fabulosas, sol todo el día. 189.900 €. F.412–41–41.
JT.C/AVINYO.
Listo vivir, 3 hab., baño, salón, cocina, terraza, muchisima luz. 102.000 €. F.412–41–41.
JT.RDA. SANT PAU.
Gran piso, 4 hab., baño, salón comedor, cocina, trastero, suel. cerámicas, listo vivir, sol todo día. 169.900 €. F.412–41–41.

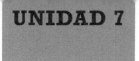

3 *Para buscar piso*

You are interested in buying a flat in Madrid. You have seen this advert and have arranged to see the flat with an estate agent.

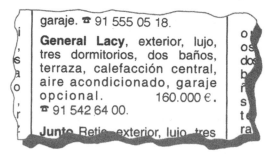

garaje. ☎ 91 555 05 18.

General Lacy, exterior, lujo, tres dormitorios, dos baños, terraza, calefacción central, aire acondicionado, garaje opcional.   160.000 €.
☎ 91 542 64 00.

Junto Retiro, exterior, lujo, tres

a Can you write the questions you would like to ask the estate agent?

E.A: **Buenas tardes.**

Tú: **................................., vengo por el anuncio del piso.**

E.A: **Sí, pase, pase.**

Tú: ¿ **......................... el piso?**

E.A: **Es muy grande y es todo exterior.**

Tú: ¿ **...................................... ?**

E.A: **Tienes dos dormitorios, comedor, cocina y baño.**

Tú: **¿Todas las habitaciones son .... ?**

E.A: **Bueno, los dormitorios sí, pero el baño es interior.**

Tú: ¿ **... ?**

E.A: **Sí, tiene ascensor.**

Tú: ¿ **... ?**

E.A: **Sí, por supuesto. Tiene calefacción central desde noviembre a marzo.**

Tú: ¿ **...................................... ?**

E.A: **Sí, tiene una terraza pequeña, al lado de la cocina.**

Tú: **Y la cocina, ¿dónde ....?**

E.A: **Al lado del comedor.**

Tú: ¿ **...................................... ?**

E.A: **No, aire acondicionado no tiene.**

b You realise that the flat is not exactly the same as it appears in the advert. Can you spot the differences?

4 *¿Ser o Estar? That's the question!*

Revising the uses of Ser *and* Estar

Complete the following sentences using the appropriate verb.

Example: **La cocina es grande y soleada.**

1 **Miguel Bosé .... actor y cantante.**
2 **Fidel Castro .... cubano.**
3 **Malaga .... en el Sur de España.**
4 **Mi casa .... moderna y original.**
5 **¿Qué hora .... ?**
6 **El sofá .... en la sala de estar.**
7 **Esta .... mi hermana Beatriz.**
8 **La parada del autobús .... enfrente del Hotel.**
9 **Galicia .... lejos de Madrid.**
10 **Toledo .... una ciudad antigua.**

5 *¿Gusta o Gustan?*

Expressing likes and dislikes

Ask the questions and then write the answers using the clues provided.

Example: **¿Te gusta la cerveza? No. Vino.**
  No, detesto la cerveza pero me encanta el vino.

  ¿Te gustan las galletas? Sí.
  Sí, me encantan.

1 ¿**................. los gatos? No. Los perros.**
  ..
2 ¿**................... la salsa? Sí.**
  ..
3 ¿**................... la comida mexicana? Sí.**
  ..
4 ¿**....................... la Opera? No. Música pop.**
  ..
5 ¿**....................... los pasteles? No. El chocolate.**
  ..

Pilar	Pepe	Ana
Me gusta la salsa.	✔	✗
No me gusta el fútbol.	✔	✗
No me gustan los gatos.	✗	✔
Me gusta la comida china.	✗	✔
Me gusta el español.	✔	✔
Me gusta el tenis.	✗	✔
No me gusta la música rock.	✗	✗
Me gustan los perros.	✔	✗
✗= no me gusta / no me gustan ✔= me gusta / me gustan		

6 ¿Los mismos gustos o gustos diferentes?

Expressing agreement or disagreement

Look at the chart above which indicates what three friends like and dislike.

How do Pepe and Ana agree or disagree with Pilar's opinions on the left hand side?

Use *A mí también, A mí no* to agree or disagree with a positive sentence and *A mí tampoco, A mí sí* as a response to a negative sentence.

7 Sentence order

Can you put these sentences in the right order?

Example: ¿al teatro Te gusta ir?
           Te gusta ir al teatro.

1 me no gustan nada los gatos

....

2 mi gusta hermano le al fútbol jugar A

....

3 ¿gusta Os música la clásica?

....

4 A padres les gusta mis comida italiana la

....

5 nosotros encanta A nos bailar

....

8 Developing your reading skills

a Read this extract from the autobiography of the Spanish film director Luis Buñuel. Look at the list below in English and decide which things Buñuel would like or dislike and explain why.

a To have lunch at one clock

   Sí, porque le gusta comer temprano.

b A rainy day in England

....

c Going on holiday to Sweden

....

d A trip to the Sahara desert

....

e A person who's always late

....

f A ban on alcohol and tobacco

....

g Reading the stock market section in the Financial Times

....

h Attending a wedding reception with 200 people

....

i Being a journalist

....

Me gusta comer temprano, acostarme y levantarme pronto. En eso soy completamente antiespañol.

Me gusta el ruido de la lluvia. Lo recuerdo como uno de los ruidos más bellos del mundo.

Me gusta verdaderamente el frío. Durante toda mi juventud, aun en lo más crudo del invierno me paseaba sin gabán, con una simple camisa y una chaqueta.

No me gustan los paises cálidos, consecuencia lógica de lo anterior. Si vivo en México es por casualidad. No me gustan el desierto ni la arena.

Me gusta la puntualidad. A decir verdad, es una manía. No recuerdo haber llegado tarde ni una sola vez en mi vida.

Adoro los bares, el alcohol y el tabaco.

No me gustan las estadísticas. Es imposible leer una página del periódico sin encontrar una. Además todas son falsas. Puedo asegurarlo.

Detesto mortalmente los banquetes y las entregas de premios.

Detesto la proliferación de información. La lectura de un periódico es la cosa más angustiosa del mundo.

Detesto la publicidad y hago todo lo posible por evitarla. La sociedad en que vivimos es totalmente publicitaria.

No me gusta la política.

96

UNIDAD 8

Objectives

Describing people
Describing your symptoms
to a doctor
Asking for advice and
understanding remedies
Giving advice

1 Revisión

Practising question forms

Complete the sentences with the appropriate words.

Example: ¿A qué hora te levantas?

1 ¿... te llamas?
2 ¿... hora sale el tren?
3 ¿... vives?
4 ¿... hermanos tienes?
5 ¿............... distancia está Zaragoza de Madrid?
6 ¿... te duele?
7 ¿... es todo?
8 ¿... es Marina? Es de Perú.
9 ¿... es esa señora?
   Es mi madre.
10 ¿... es tu hermana?

2 ¿Cómo es?

Describing people

Read the sentences and match the descriptions with the appropriate picture.

a Es alto y delgado. Tiene el pelo rubio, corto y liso.

b Es bajo y un poco gordo. Tiene el pelo negro y rizado. Tiene barba.

c Es alto y delgado. Tiene el pelo negro y rizado. Tiene bigote.

d Es bajito y delgado. Es moreno y tiene el pelo corto y rizado.

e Es alto y un poco gordo. Tiene el pelo negro y rizado. Tiene bigote.

f Es bajito y un poco gordo. Es rubio y tiene el pelo liso. Tiene barba.

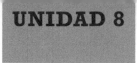

3 *Adjetivos*

Can you find the opposites of the following adjectives? Take into account whether the adjectives are feminine or masculine, singular or plural.

Example: **1 alta – baja**

1 alta ....

2 simpáticos ....

3 feo ....

4 aburrida ....

5 viejo ....

6 inteligentes ....

7 gordo ....

8 rubio ....

9 tímidas ....

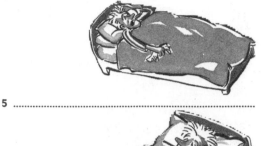

5 ....

6 ....

4 *En el médico*

a What would you say to the doctor?

Médico: **¿Qué le pasa?**

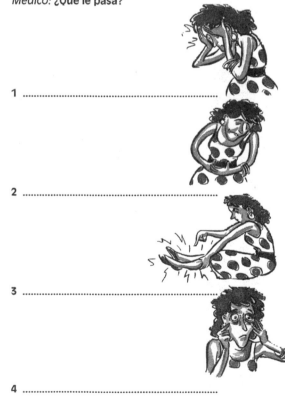

1 ....

2 ....

3 ....

4 ....

7 ....

8 ....

b Which remedies would you suggest to a friend suffering from the pains and illnesses in Activity a)?

Example: **Tienes que tomar una aspirina / debes tomar una aspirina.**

5 *Busca al intruso*

Find the odd-one-out.

a médico   estantería   hospital   enfermera

b cabeza   barriga   crema   mano

c jarabe   gotas   resfriado   pastillas

d estómago   garganta   ojos   medicina

e quemadura de sol   comprimidos   insolación   deshidratación

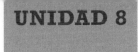

6 Vida sana

Giving suggestions

This is the advice and the recommendations that well-known magazines give to their readers to help them lead healthy lives.

a Read the article and classify the positive and negative things in the box that will affect your health.

> "Si quiere llevar una vida sana, es necesario seguir una dieta equilibrada: comer mucha fruta y verdura. Es imprescindible no comer muchas grasas ni dulces. Es recomendable usar aceite de oliva. Es muy importante beber agua, como mínimo un litro y medio cada día. Está demostrado que el alcohol en dosis moderadas es bueno para la salud pero no es conveniente beber mucho. Es imprescindible no fumar. Es necesario combatir el estrés, por eso es muy importante hacer ejercicio y dormir bastante. Si sigue nuestros consejos verá mejorar su calidad de vida."

Cosas positivas para la salud	Cosas negativas
Comer mucha fruta y verdura	No comer muchas grasas ni dulces

b Use the information from Activity a) and write suggestions to help people lead healthier lives.

> *Example:* 'Tienes que comer mucha fruta y verdura. / Debes comer mucha fruta.'
> 'No tienes que comer muchas grasas ni dulces. / No debes comer grasas ni dulces.'

7 ¿Ser o Estar?

Fill in the gaps using the appropriate verb, *ser* or *estar*.

Carmela .... española. .... alta y delgada. .... periodista. Esta semana no trabaja porque .... enferma. .... muy aburrida, porque está sola. Aurora es su amiga y .... periodista también. Hoy ,.......... jueves y Aurora va a visitar a Carmela.
Carmela .... en la cama.

Aurora: Hola Carmela. ¿Qué tal ....?

Carmela: Hola. .... mejor, pero .... un poco cansada.

Aurora: Mira, te traigo unas galletas. ¿Quieres tomar algo caliente? ¿Un café o una manzanilla?

Carmela: Un café con leche, mejor.

Aurora: Vale, ahora mismo lo preparo ...

UNIDAD 9

Objectives

Expressing likes and dislikes about activities and hobbies
Ordering drinks and snacks
Saying dates

1 Actividades

Revising your vocabulary

Match the words and expressions below with the appropriate verb.

al fútbol	al cine
la compra	al tenis
al parque	a tomar unas copas
montañismo	la cama
de compras	de copas

Example: Ir de copas

ir	hacer	jugar

2 La media naranja

a Eva is looking for *(busca)* a suitable partner and this is her classified ad in a magazine. Fill in the gaps with the words below.

me gusta	me encantan
soltera	serio
correr	entre

hombre y educado.

♥ ♥ ♥ ♥ ♥ ♥ ♥ ♥ ♥

Profesional ..... de 32 años, busca hombre ..... y educado, ... 30 y 40 años ..... jugar al tenis y ..... También ..... los animales. Ap. 2801

♥ ♥ ♥ ♥ ♥ ♥ ♥ ♥

Profesional ..... de 32 años, busca

b Luis is also looking for a partner. Here you have his details and the description of his ideal *media naranja*. Write an ad for him.

arquitecto
divorciado
sensible
culto
40 años
viajar
los niños
el campo

mujer sensible y divertida 30 – 40 años

c Write your own ad looking for your *media naranja*.

3 Problemas de amor

All these people suffer from unrequited love. Can you say why?

Example: A Luisa le gusta Juan pero a Juan le gusta María.

28

4 Fechas perdidas

Margarita has lost her address book. She is
on the phone asking her sister the family's
birthday dates. What are the answers?

¿Qué día es el cumpleaños
de la tía Clara?

Clara, 3/2/1935

¿Y el cumpleaños del tío
Pascual?

Pascual, 13/7/1930

¿Y qué día es el cumpleaños
de Rosi?

Rosi, 12/12/1963

¿Y el santo?

31/8

¿Y el cumpleaños de Ramón?

Ramón, 2/11/1970

¿Y el santo?

1/5

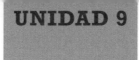

5 En el bar

a These sentences are likely to be heard in a bar. Can you complete them?

1 ¿Tienen algo ....?

2 ¿Algo ....?

3 ¿Cuánto ....?

4 ¿Qué van a ....?

b Match these answers with the questions above.

a) Un café y un vino tinto.   ☐

b) Son 7,20 euros.   ☐

c) No, nada más.   ☐

d) Hay bocadillos de jamón, queso y tortilla.   ☐

c Now put the questions and answers from Activities a) and b) in order to build up a dialogue. Add these other sentences.

Uno de queso para mí.
Aquí tiene, gracias.
A usted. Adiós.

6 Tomando algo en el bar

Practising your dialogue skills

Look at the picture below. Complete the dialogue taking into account what the people want to order.

Camarero: **¿Qué van a tomar?**

Cliente 1: ....

Cliente 2: ....

¿ .... ?

Camarero: **Sí, hay bocadillos de jamón, queso, mortadela, chorizo, calamares ...**

Cliente 1: ....

Cliente 2: ....

(Five minutes later)

Camarero: **Aquí tienen. El de queso, ¿para quién es?**

Cliente 1: **Para** .... **El de jamón** ....

Cliente 2: ¿ ....?

Camarero: **9,35 euros.**

Cliente: **Aquí tiene. Gracias y hasta mañana.**

Camarero: **Adiós. Muchas gracias.**

café con leche, bocadillo de jamón

cerveza, queso

UNIDAD 10
Objectives

Reading and understanding tickets
Enquiring about train timetables,
prices and services
Practising irregular verbs and
prepositions
Writing skills: writing an informal
invitation letter giving information
about how to get to a place

1 Un billete de tren

Reading and understanding a train ticket

Look at this ticket and decide whether the
sentences below are true or false.

1 Es un billete para Granada.

2 El billete cuesta 32,50 euros.

3 Es un billete de primera clase.

4 El billete es para el día 25 de febrero.

5 El viaje dura seis horas y media.

6 Es un billete de fumadores.

7 Este billete se paga con tarjeta de
crédito.

2 Preposiciones

Practising the use of prepositions

Complete the sentences with these
prepositions: *en, a, de, para, con.*
In one of the sentences no preposition is
needed.

Example: **Normalmente vuelvo a casa a las 9.**

1 *A:* **Normalmente voy al trabajo ..... coche.**

  B: **Pues yo voy ..... pie.**

2 **Hay una estación ..... el centro de la ciudad.**

3 *A:* **¿Cómo puedo ir ..... Málaga ..... Córdoba?**

  B: **Puede ir ..... tren o ..... autobús.**

4 **¿..... qué hora sale el próximo tren ..... León?**

5 **Quisiera un billete ..... ida y vuelta ..... Alicante.**

6 **Quiero salir ..... el lunes 23.**

7 **¿Va a pagar ..... cheque o ..... efectivo?**

8 **¿Se puede pagar ..... tarjeta de crédito?**

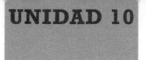

3 En la oficina de turismo

Practising your dialogue skills

Can you think what the questions are for these answers?

a ....
b ....
c ....
d ....
e ....

1 **El tren sale a las 8.**
2 **No, sólo en efectivo.**
3 **No, aquí no se puede fumar.**
4 **Puede ir en tren o en avión.**
5 **Prefiero el tren; es más cómodo.**

4 Verbos irregulares

Practising irregular verbs

Complete the sentences with the appropriate person of the verbs in brackets. Use the present tense.

Example: **Carlos, ¿a qué hora (empezar) ..... a trabajar?**
Carlos, ¿a qué hora empiezas a trabajar?

1 A: **Oye, Juan, ¿cuántos hermanos (tener)...................................?**

   B: **(tener) .... cuatro hermanos.**

2 A: **¿Qué (preferir) .... señor Castillos, té o café?**

   B: **Un café, por favor.**

3 A: **No me gusta el coche, (preferir) .... el tren.**

   B: **¿Sí? Pues nosotros (preferir) .... el coche. Es más rápido.**

4 A: **¿A qué hora (volver) .... los niños de la escuela?**

   B: **Marcos (volver) .... a las 5.30 y Eva a las 6.00.**

5 A: **¿Qué te pasa?**

   B: **Me (doler) .... la cabeza.**

   A: **¿Por qué no (acostarse) ....?**

6 A: **Julio, ¿a qué hora (empezar) .... la película?**

   B: **A las nueve.**

7 – **Pepe, ¿(querer) .... tomar un café?**

8 – **Juan y yo no (poder) .... ir a la reunión de vecinos porque (empezar) .... a trabajar a las 8.30.**

B: **No (poder) .... Carlos (venir) .... a cenar esta noche.**

5 Una invitación

Revising grammar and vocabulary

Pablo is writing to his friend Miguel, inviting Miguel to come over and visit him in Sevilla. Complete the letter with these missing words:

salen   coger   es   es   vienes   dura   puedo

Querido Miguel,

¿Por qué no ..... a visitarme a Sevilla?

Puedes ..... el AVE, el tren de alta velocidad, y en un momento estás aquí, porque el viaje sólo ..... dos horas y media. Y no ..... nada caro: un billete de ida y vuelta ..... sólo 124€.

Los trenes ..... todos los días a las 9, las 11, las 13 y 14 horas y yo ..... ir a la estación y recogerte. ¿Qué te parece mi idea? Anímate y vente para Sevilla.

Un abrazo,

Pablo

6 *Una carta para un amigo*

Practising your writing skills

Write a similar letter to a friend using the information in the box below. Don't forget to encourage your friend to visit you, *Anímate y vente para ....* Don't forget either to give him/her *abrazos* (a hug).

Visitar	Cáceres
Horario de trenes	Salidas a las 09.00 y las 12.00
Duración del viaje	Cuatro horas
Precio del billete	21 €
Tipo de tren	El Talgo, muy cómodo.

7 *Reservar un billete por teléfono*

Practising your dialogue skills

You are in Madrid and you need to fly to Bilbao on the 28th. You have an important appointment at 14.30. Phone your travel agent and book a ticket.

Ag: **Viajes Luna, ¿Dígame?**

Tú: **Buenos días, ...**

Ag: **¿Para que día?**

Tú: **...**

Ag: **Hay un vuelo que sale a las 9, otro a la 1 y el último a las 5.30 de la tarde.**

Tú: **¿ .... ?**

Ag: **Dura unos 50 minutos.**

Tú: **Entonces, ...**

Ag: **¿Ida y vuelta?**

Tú: **.............. ida. ¿ .... ?**

Ag: **Son 145,21 euros.**

Tú: **Vale.**

Ag: **¿Va a pagar con tarjeta de crédito?**

Tú: **Sí, ... de crédito.**

Ag: **¿Me da el número de su tarjeta?**

Tú: **Es el ....**

Ag: **Vale, ya tiene su billete. Se lo enviamos por Correo.**

Tú: **Vale, de acuerdo. Muchas gracias.**

Ag: **Adiós.**

Tú: **Adiós.**

8 *EL tren AVE*

Understanding transport information

El Ave is the latest and fastest Spanish train. It links Madrid and Sevilla in just two and a half hours. Read the information about the discounts offered to customers using the AVE and say whether the sentences below are true or false.

1 **Si vas a Sevilla el lunes y vuelves 4 días más tarde, tienes un descuento del 20%.** ☐

2 **Si vas a Sevilla el lunes y vuelves a Madrid el martes te hacen un descuento del 30%.** ☐

3 **Los niños entre 6 y 11 años sólo pagan el 40% del precio normal.** ☐

4 **Un niño de 6 meses tiene que pagar el 40% también.** ☐

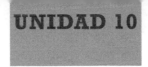

SERVICIOS ÚTILES

Los servicios de RENFE

EN ALGUNAS OCASIONES, EL FERROCARRIL ES UN MEDIO DE TRANSPORTE MÁS RÁPIDO Y ECONÓMICO QUE EL COCHE

Ahorre con el AVE

Disfrutar de los servicios del AVE resulta ahora más asequible a su bolsillo: ¡Atentos a estas opciones de viaje!:

• Ida y Vuelta: si adquiere un billete de ida y vuelta cerrado y realiza la vuelta en los 15 días siguientes a la ida, podrá beneficiarse de un 20% de descuento sobre la tarifa nacional.

• Día (Ida y Vuelta): Puede ir y volver en el mismo día con un descuento del 30% en todos los trenes AVE, excepto en Lanzaderas.

• Infantil: Los niños entre 4 y 11 años disfrutarán de una reducción del 40% sobre la tarifa general. Los niños de menos de 4 años no pagan billete.

UNIDAD 11

Objectives

Booking a room in a hotel
Checking in
Making complaints
Finding out what's on

1 Reservar una habitación por teléfono

Practising your dialogue skills

a You are phoning the Hotel Meliá to book a room. Use the information in the picture and complete the dialogue with the receptionist.

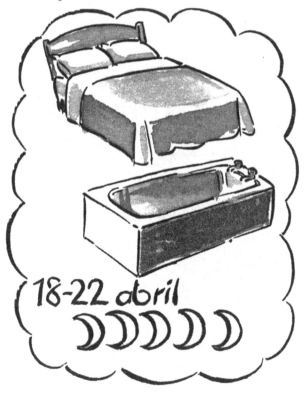

18-22 abril

R: **Hotel Meliá. Dígame.**

Tú: .... **con cama doble.**

R: **¿Para cuántas noches?**

Tú: ....

R: **¿Para qué días?**

Tú: ....

R: **¿La quiere con baño o con ducha?**

Tú: ....

R: **¿A nombre de quién?**

Tú: ....

¿ .... ?

R: **Son 85€ por noche.**

Tú: ¿ .... ?

R: **Sí, el desayuno está incluído.**

Tú: **Vale, muy bien.**

R: **De acuerdo, le hago la reserva. Una habitación doble con baño desde el día 18 al 22 de abril.**

Tú: **Muy bien, muchas gracias. Adiós.**

R: **Hasta pronto.**

b You have arrived at the Hotel Meliá. Confirm your reservation with the receptionist.

You: *Say that you have booked a room.*

....

R: **¿A nombre de quién?**

You: *Say your name.*

....

R: **Sí, aquí tengo su reserva. Me firma y me da su pasaporte.**

You: **Sí, como no.**

You: *Ask what time breakfast is.*

....

R: **De 8 a 10 de la mañana.**

You: *Ask whether there is a chemist near the hotel.*

....

R: **Sí, está muy cerca, enfrente mismo del hotel.**

You: *Say thank you.*

....

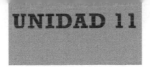

2 *El libro de reclamaciones*

In Spain it is compulsory that all hotels have a 'Complaints Book' where customers are entitled to write a complaint if the service has not lived up to your expectations. You have recently stayed in a hotel where everything went wrong. You are upset and decide to make a complaint.

Existe un Libro de Reclamaciones a disposición del cliente

Write a complaint. The information in the bubbles will give you the reasons for your complaints.

Example: **Quisiera protestar por las malas condiciones de la habitación número 28. La ducha no funciona** ....

....

3 *Los servicios del Hotel*

Can you remember the name of these services? Write them down.

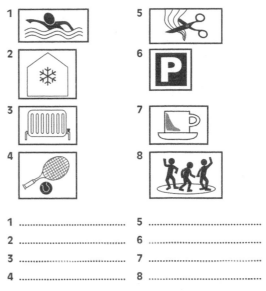

1 .... 5 ....
2 .... 6 ....
3 .... 7 ....
4 .... 8 ....

4 *Reservar una habitación por carta*

Practising your writing skills

You would like to book a double room from 15th to 30th of June, with two beds and with a bath. Enquire about the following services: air conditioning, tennis court and swimming pool.

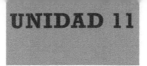
5 Vocabulario

Revising your vocabulary

Complete the grid with the appropriate words. You should find the surname of a Spanish writer vertically.

1 Día de la semana.

2 Lo contrario de *nunca*.

3 Bebida alcohólica.

4 Habitación para una persona.

5 Parte de la casa.

6 Una mujer de Inglaterra es ...

7 El hermano de tu madre es tu ...

8 Buenos días. Tengo una habitación ...

9 Lo contrario de *limpio*.

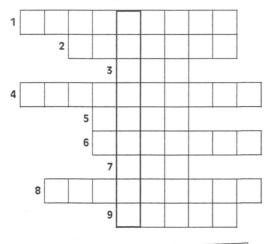

6 ¡De vacaciones!

Practising your reading skills

Read the information below and choose the most appropriate 'Parador' for the following people:

1 Una familia con dos niños. Les gusta la playa y el sol.

2 Una pareja joven. Les gusta la montaña y hacer excursiones.

3 Dos estudiantes de Arte. Les encanta la arquitectura.

4 Un matrimonio mayor. Quieren un lugar tranquilo para descansar. Les gusta mucho pescar.

5 Una señora que quiere visitar una ciudad antigua y monumental y estar en el centro.

PARADORES
Hoteles desde 1928

Parador de Bielsa ★★★

El Parador se encuentra al fondo del maravilloso Valle de Pineta a 14 km de Bielsa, capital del alto Cinca, junto al nacimiento de dicho río y a los pies de Las Tres Sorores (Monte Perdido, Cilindro y Soum de Ramond, picos que superan los 3.350 metros de altitud). Por su ubicación es un lugar ideal para visitar el Parque Nacional de Ordesa y Monte Perdido, hacer montañismo y toda clase de excursiones por los bellos parajes que le circundan. Asimismo la caza y la pesca son muy abundantes en la zona. Desde este lugar se pueden visitar los bonitos pueblos cercanos con sus iglesias del siglo XIII dotadas de retablos de gran interés.

Valle de Pineta 22350 BIELSA (Huesca)
Tel.: (974) 50 10 11 Fax: (974) 50 11 88

Parador de ALMAGRO ★★★★

El Parador ha sido edificado sobre el antiguo convento franciscano de Santa Catalina, construido por D. Jerónimo Davila y de la Cueva, interesante figura del siglo XVI. Es imprescindible la visita a la Plaza Mayor y al Corral de Comedias, conservado como en el Siglo de Oro. Ciudad Real, a 22 km, con su Catedral, cuya construcción se inició en el año 1531, y la iglesia de San Pedro del siglo XIV, así como la localidad de El Viso del Marqués con un magnífico palacio del siglo XVI, son lugares dignos de ser visitados.

Ronda de San Francisco, 31
13270 ALMAGRO (Ciudad Real)
Tel.: (926) 86 01 00 Fax: (926) 86 01 50

CENTRAL DE RESERVAS:
Requena 3, 28013, Madrid   Tfnos Centralita: (91) 559 0978
Reservas (91) 559 0069   Fax Reservas: (91) 559 32 33
Fax General: (91) 559 20 42

PARADORES
Hoteles desde 1928

Parador de AIGUABLAVA ★★★★

Edificio moderno de estilo funcional situado en la punta D'es Muts, una pequeña península que domina un hermoso panorama de calas y playas rodeadas de pinares. Próximo a Bagur, con su castillo medieval, y Pals, rodeado de murallas.

Platja d'Aiguablava
17255 BAGUR (Girona) Tel.: (972) 62 21 62 Fax: (972) 62 21 66 Télex: 56275

7 Una invitación

a A friend of yours phones to invite you to a concert. Can you find out all the details about it?

Tú: **Dígame.**

Pepe: **Oye, tengo entradas para un concierto. ¿Quieres venir?**

Tú: ¿ .... ?

Pepe: **Es música rock.**

Tú: ¿ .... ?

Pepe: **En la Sala Universal.**

Tú: ¿ .... ?

Pepe: **El viernes próximo.**

Tú: ¿ .... ?

Pepe: **A las 10 de la noche.**

Tú: ¿ .... ?

Pepe: **No te preocupes. Tengo dos invitaciones.**

Tú: ¿ .... ?

Pepe: **En la Plaza de Roma.**

Tú: **Vale. Muchas gracias.**

Pepe: **De nada.**

b Now read this advert and make a similar dialogue with the information about the concert.

CONCIERTO
HOMENAJE A PABLO
SARASATE

Auditorio Nacional de Música.
Sala Sinfónica.
Miércoles 19 de Octubre, 20.00 horas.

Orquesta Sinfónica de Chile.
Director Invitado: Odón Alonso.
Solista: Silvia Marcovici.

Localidades a la venta en las taquillas de Auditorio
Nacional, Av. Palacio de la Moneda.

....
....
....
....
....
....
....
....
....
....

UNIDAD 12

Objectives

Relating past events
Writing a postcard saying what you did during your holidays

1 ¿Qué tipo de vacaciones?

Practising your reading skills

a Read the extracts from a holiday brochure below and decide which holiday these people chose.

Ramiro es profesor de arte y tiene un especial interés por la arquitectura y la arqueología. ☐

Ester es muy activa y aficionada a los deportes al aire libre. ☐

Ramón es un hombre muy ocupado. Cuando va de vacaciones quiere un lugar tranquilo para pasar tiempo con su familia. No le gustan mucho los deportes. ☐

1 *Tenerife.* Oferta de una semana (del 9 al 16) al sur de Tenerife, por 450 euros. Está incluído el vuelo, los traslados de aeropuerto, el alojamiento en régimen de pensión completa y el seguro.
En la isla es conveniente alquilar un coche para subir al Teide y visitar Masca, Taganana, Icod de los Vinos y el valle de la Orotava. Si lo que se busca es un poco de animación nocturna, el mejor punto es el Puerto de la Cruz. A la hora de hacer compras, la opción más acertada es acercarse a Santa Cruz de Tenerife y visitar los almacenes Maya, junto a la plaza de la Candelaria – a la vez se da un paseo por el centro de la ciudad – e Ikea (a las afueras). En cuestión de paladar, los mejores restaurantes también están salpicados por toda la isla. Desde El Drago (en Tegueste), hasta Los Arcos (en Tacoronte).
Viajes Barceló: 902 20 04 00.

2 *México.* Ruinas mayas. Se trata de un circuito en autocar por las ruinas mayas de Akumal, Tulum, Coba, Chichen Itzá, Uxmal, Mérida, Izamal, a lo largo de la península mexicana del Yucatán. El viaje comienza el sábado 8 de abril y finaliza el día 16. El precio es 1.280 euros e incluye el vuelo a Cancún, el alojamiento y desayuno en hoteles a lo largo del recorrido, la entrada a todos los museos y monumentos y el seguro.
Organiza Iberojet

3 *Cáceres.* Cinco días de multi-aventura (del 12 al 17) en Villasbuenas de Gata (Cáceres). El programa incluye excursiones a caballo, pesca deportiva, bicicleta de montaña, senderismo, natación … Los 285 euros también dan derecho al alojamiento y al seguro. Se pueden hacer excursiones a Portugal (Serra da Estala y parque Serrada Malcata), a Salamanca (Ciudad Rodrigo, La Alberca, sierra de Francia) y al parque natural de Monfragüe y Las Urdes.
News Actividades 91 31 40 28

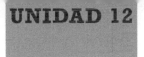

	Duración del viaje	Transporte	Alojamiento	Precio
Tenerife				
México				
Cáceres				

b Read the holiday brochure again and complete the table with the information required.

c What activities did each of these people do on their holidays?

Example: **Ester montó en bici.**

2 Una postal desde México

a Ramón went to México and after his holidays he wrote a letter to a friend telling him about his holiday there. Fill in the gaps with the missing verbs.

> Querido Paco,
> La semana pasada (estar) .... de vacaciones en México. ¡Fue fenomenal! (Llegar) .... a Cancún el día 9 y (irse) .... a Tulum que está a unos 130 km. Hay unas ruinas mayas junto a una playa preciosa en la costa caribeña. Al día siguiente (tomar) .... el autobús y (visitar) .... la ciudad maya de Chichen Itzá, que es una de las más grandes y mejor conservadas del Yucatán. (Subir) .... a la pirámide de Kukuleán. Por la tarde (volver) .... a Cancún y (tomar) .... unas copas en el jardín del Hotel. El martes al mediodía (comer) .... en un restaurante excelente y después (ir) .... de compras a un mercado de artesanos. En fin, que lo (pasar) .... muy bien ...

b Now write a similar letter from Ester to a friend. Ester went to Cáceres. You can use the information provided in the brochure in Activity 1.

3 Practising your dialogue skills

Carlos and Patricia are talking about last weekend. Complete the dialogue with the appropriate questions.

Carlos: ¿Qué tal el fin de semana?

Patricia: **Bien, nada especial. El sábado fui al cine y cené fuera.**

Carlos: ¿ .... ?

Patricia: **El Señor de los Anillos.**

Carlos: ¿ .... ?

Patricia: **No mucho. No es una película demasiado interesante.**

Carlos: ¿ .... ?

Patricia: **En un restaurante italiano que está en la calle Huertas.**

Carlos: ¿ .... ?

Patricia: **Muy bien, pero un poco caro.**

Carlos: ¿ .... el domingo?

Patricia: **Nada, nada en absoluto. Dormir y ver la tele.**

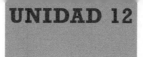

4 ¿Cuándo?

Revising your vocabulary: expressions of time

a Complete the expressions of time below with the appropriate letters.

```
_l  v_r_n_  p_s_d_
_y_r
_n_ch_
_nt__y_r
_l  m_s  p_s_d_
l_  s_m_n_  p_s_d_
_n  d_c_  _mbr_
_l  d_m_ng_
```

b Can you remember what you did on those dates? Write sentences using the expressions of time from Activity a) and your own information.

Example: **El verano pasado fui de vacaciones a Bretaña.**

5 Las gemelas (The twin sisters)

Practising the past tense: plural forms

a The police think the twin sisters robbed the Banco de León last Monday. The pictures show the sisters' version of what they did that day. Can you guess what they said to the police?

Example: **El lunes nos levantamos a las 9.**

b However, after some witnesses were questioned, the police found out new details about what the sisters had done. Write a report with the new evidence.

Example: **A las 10.30 no hicieron la compra.**
Compraron un billete de avión.

6 *La boda real*

Practising your reading skills

In 1995 Infanta Elena, eldest daughter of the Spanish King Juan Carlos I, was married in Seville. Here are some extracts from the Spanish newspapers about the event. Put them in order. The first paragraph is given to you.

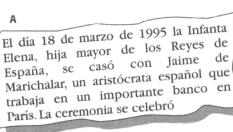

A

El día 18 de marzo de 1995 la Infanta Elena, hija mayor de los Reyes de España, se casó con Jaime de Marichalar, un aristócrata español que trabaja en un importante banco en París. La ceremonia se celebró

B

pasaron su luna de miel en Lanzarote, visitaron varios países europeos y finalmente fueron a Australia, donde practicaron deportes náuticos.

C

y casi mil millones de espectadores la vieron en sus casas. Después de la ceremonia los invitados comieron en los Reales Alcázares de Sevilla. El menú consistió de

D

del mundo del arte, la política y los medios de comunicación. La ceremonia, que duró 75 minutos, fue retransmitida en directo a medio mundo

E

en la catedral de Sevilla. Más de 1.500 invitados asistieron a la boda, entre ellos destacados miembros de familias reales y personajes famosos

F

dos platos, uno de carne y otro de pescado, un postre, tarta nupcial y vinos españoles. Los novios

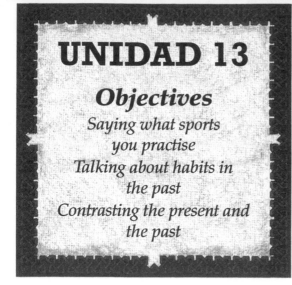

UNIDAD 13

Objectives

*Saying what sports
you practise
Talking about habits in
the past
Contrasting the present and
the past*

1 Los deportes

Revising your vocabulary

Complete the crossword with the names of
the sports illustrated.

▶ ACROSS   ▼ DOWN

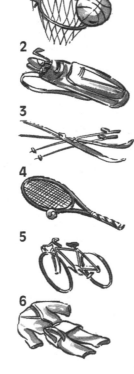

2 Haciendo deporte

a Can you write ten expressions with one item
from each box?

jugar	a	baloncesto
montar	al	tenis
hacer	en	caballo
practicar	Ø (nothing)	bicicleta
		voleivol
		golf
		judo
		'footing'
		squash
		gimnasia

1 *jugar al tenis* ....   6 ....
2 ....   7 ....
3 ....   8 ....
4 ....   9 ....
5 .... 10 ....

b Which sports do you practise?

42

3 ¿Llevas una vida sana?

Test your reading and comprehension skills

Do you lead a healthy life? Answer the
questionnaire and find out!

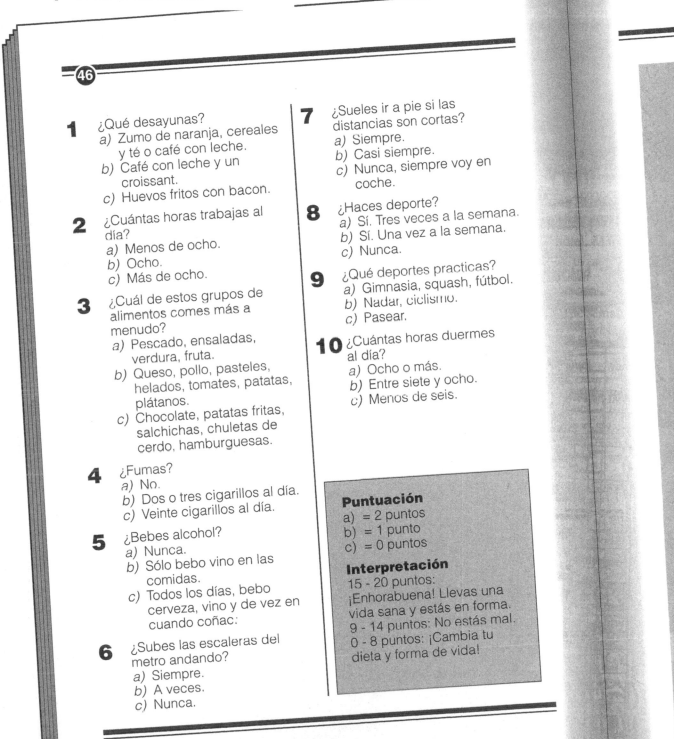

46

1 ¿Qué desayunas?
a) Zumo de naranja, cereales
y té o café con leche.
b) Café con leche y un
croissant.
c) Huevos fritos con bacon.

2 ¿Cuántas horas trabajas al
día?
a) Menos de ocho.
b) Ocho.
c) Más de ocho.

3 ¿Cuál de estos grupos de
alimentos comes más a
menudo?
a) Pescado, ensaladas,
verdura, fruta.
b) Queso, pollo, pasteles,
helados, tomates, patatas,
plátanos.
c) Chocolate, patatas fritas,
salchichas, chuletas de
cerdo, hamburguesas.

4 ¿Fumas?
a) No.
b) Dos o tres cigarillos al día.
c) Veinte cigarillos al día.

5 ¿Bebes alcohol?
a) Nunca.
b) Sólo bebo vino en las
comidas.
c) Todos los días, bebo
cerveza, vino y de vez en
cuando coñac.

6 ¿Subes las escaleras del
metro andando?
a) Siempre.
b) A veces.
c) Nunca.

7 ¿Sueles ir a pie si las
distancias son cortas?
a) Siempre.
b) Casi siempre.
c) Nunca, siempre voy en
coche.

8 ¿Haces deporte?
a) Sí. Tres veces a la semana.
b) Sí. Una vez a la semana.
c) Nunca.

9 ¿Qué deportes practicas?
a) Gimnasia, squash, fútbol.
b) Nadar, ciclismo.
c) Pasear.

10 ¿Cuántas horas duermes
al día?
a) Ocho o más.
b) Entre siete y ocho.
c) Menos de seis.

Puntuación
a) = 2 puntos
b) = 1 punto
c) = 0 puntos

Interpretación
15 - 20 puntos:
¡Enhorabuena! Llevas una
vida sana y estás en forma.
9 - 14 puntos: No estás mal.
0 - 8 puntos: ¡Cambia tu
dieta y forma de vida!

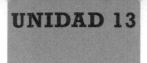

4 Antes y ahora

Testing your listening skills

 Listen to the tape from Unit 13, Track 4, of your Coursebook.

a Write down a list with the times you can hear.

....
....
....
....

b Listen again and write down what Miguel used to do at those hours.

Example: **A las 9 se levantaba**

....
....
....
....

5 La lotería

In the chart below you have information about Ana and Pedro when they were in their twenties. They were poor and life was difficult, but they had a good time. Three years ago they won the lottery. They have plenty of money. Life is easy. And they still have a good time.

a Read the information in the chart and write sentences about their life then and now.

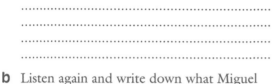
Example: **Cuando tenían 20 años trabajaban mucho pero ahora trabajan poco.**

....
....
....
....
....

b Imagine you are old and rich. Write about your life now, and your life when you were young.

Cuando tenían 20 años	Ahora
ser pobres	ser ricos
trabajar mucho	no trabajar mucho
vivir en un piso pequeño	vivir en una casa con piscina
comer en restaurantes baratos	comer en restaurantes caros
no ir de vacaciones	ir de vacaciones al extranjero
ningún deporte	hacer gimnasia y jugar al tenis
tener muchos amigos	todavía tener muchos amigos
no tener coche	tener dos coches

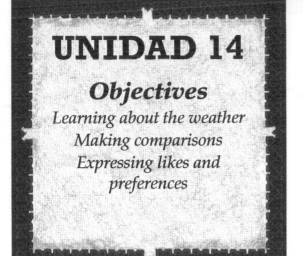

Objectives

Learning about the weather
Making comparisons
Expressing likes and
preferences

1 Un poco de revisión: vocabulario

Revising vocabulary related to the weather

a Match the pictures with the words. (Some pictures go with more than one word.)

sol despejado nevando helada niebla viento nublado calor neblina lloviendo temperaturas altas frío cubierto

b Classify the words in Activity a) into these three groups, depending on the verb which goes with them.

Hace	Hay	Está

 c Listen to the audio material in the coursebook, section *Un paso más*, Track 8, and listen again to the weather broadcast. How many of the words above can you hear? Tick the words when you hear them.

2 ¿Qué tiempo hizo ayer?

Practising your dialogue skills

a Marta lives in Valparaíso, Chile. She is telephoning her friend Julia who lives in Zamora, in Spain. Fill in the gaps to complete the conversation.

Marta: ¿Julia? Hola, ... Marta. ¿Cómo .... ?

Julia: Muy bien, ¿y tú? ¿Qué tal en Valparaíso?

Marta: Es precioso y hoy .... un tiempo buenísimo. Esta mañana fui a la playa. ¿Qué tal por Zamora?

Julia: Por aquí como siempre. Hoy .... lloviendo y ayer .... mucho frío; sol, pero mucho frío.

Marta: Pues aquí ayer .... lloviendo por la mañana pero por la tarde .... sol.

b Now write a paragraph comparing the weather in Zamora and Valparaíso based on the information in the dialogue.

3 El tiempo en Europa

a What are the names of the countries on the map opposite?

1 ......*Italia*...... 5 ....

2 .... 6 ....

3 .... 7 ....

4 .... 8 ....

b Can you tell what the weather is like in Europe according to the map?

1 ....

2 ....

3 ....

4 ....

5 ....

6 ....

7 ....

8 ....

4 ¿Quién es quién?

Making comparisons

Read the sentences below to find out who is who.

El más alto tiene 36 años.

El más bajo se llama Enrique.

Juan es más alto que Pedro.

Juan es dos años menor que el más alto.

Luis tiene 5 años más que Enrique.

Pedro es 6 años mayor que Juan.

Nombre: .... **Nombre:** ....

Edad: .... **Edad:** ....

Nombre: .... **Nombre:** ....

Edad: .... **Edad:** ....

5 ¿Tú qué opinas?

Making comparisons and expressing likes and preferences

Look at the pictures and say which one you like best and why.

Example: **Julia Roberts es la que más me gusta porque es más atractiva que Jane Fonda. Prefiero el coche porque es más cómodo que el tren.**

....

....

6 **invierno** **verano**

....

....

6 Dos países

Practising your reading skills: Comparing statistics

a Do you think the statements below are True or False?

1 **Hay menos universidades en Bolivia.** ☐

2 **Colombia tiene menos habitantes que Bolivia.** ☐

3 **Bolivia es más grande que Colombia.** ☐

Now read the texts and check your answers.

b Now write some comparative sentences about the two countries.

....

....

....

....

....

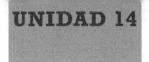

Latinoamérica en cifras

Bolivia

Extensión: 1 098.581 km²
Población: 8.140.352
Población urbana: 61%
Densidad de población: 7 habitantes por km²
Esperanza de vida: hombres: 61.9 años mujeres: 65.3 años
Universidades: 25
Exportaciones: 1.033 millones de dólares
Importaciones: 1.227 millones de dólares
Kilómetros de carreteras: 52.216 km

Colombia

Extensión: 1.138.7914 km²
Población: 41.539.000
Población urbana: 74%
Densidad de población: 37 habitantes por km²
Esperanza de vida: hombres: 69.2 años mujeres: 75.3 años
Universidades: 77
Exportaciones: 13.040 millones de dólares
Importaciones: 11.539 millones de dólares
Kilómetros de carreteras: 106.600 km

UNIDAD 15

Objectives

Talking about the past:
biographical information about
yourself and others
Expressing duration
Practising your reading and
writing skills

1 El pasado

Practising the past tense: focus on form

a Complete the table with the appropriate verb form as in the examples.

b Now write five sentences about yourself using five past tenses from Activity a).

....
....
....
....
....

	Yo	Tú	El/Ella/Usted
Pasar	pasé		
Estudiar		estudiaste	
Casarse			se casó
Divorciarse	me divorcié		
Nacer	nací		
Conocer		conociste	
Vivir			vivió
Tener		tuviste	
Ir/Ser	fui		

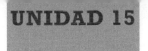
2 *Un cantante muy famoso*

Practising your reading skills: reading a biography

a Julio Iglesias is a very well-known singer but how much do you know about him? Read the sentences below and tick the box according to your opinions.

1 **Julio Iglesias nació en Madrid.** ☐

2 **Jugó al fútbol con el Real Madrid antes de empezar a cantar.** ☐

3 **Vivió en Gran Bretaña cuando era joven.** ☐

4 **Representó a España en el Festival de Eurovisión.** ☐

5 **Se casó dos veces.** ☐

6 **Tiene cuatro hijos.** ☐

b Now read Julio Iglesias' biography and confirm your opinions.

c Read the biography again and answer these questions.

1 **¿Cuánto tiempo lleva Julio Iglesias cantando?**

....

2 **¿Cuál era la profesión de su padre?**

....

3 **¿Por qué abandonó el fútbol?**

....

4 **¿En qué año se divorció?**

....

Julio Iglesias

1. El 23 Septiembre, Julio Iglesias cumplirá 60 años. En los 35 años que lleva dedicado a las canción ha vendido más de 250 milliones de discos y ha grabado alrededor de 75.

2. El cantante nació en la clínica madrileña donde ejercía como ginecólogo su padre, el doctor Julio Iglesias Puga. Estudió la carrera de Derecho.

3. Fue guardameta juvenil y aficionado en el Real Madrid, hasta que un accidente de automóvil paralizó sus piernas dos años y le separó definitivamente del fútbol.

4. Durante la convalecencia se aficionó a tocar la guitarra y a cantar. Más tarde, estudiando inglés en el Reino Unido, cantó en algunos *pubs*.

5. En 1968 ganó el X Festival de la Canción de Benidorm con *La vida sigue igual*. Después protagonizó la película del mismo título.

6. En 1970 representó a España en el Festival de Eurovisión con su canción *Gwendoline*, que quedó clasificada entre las cinco primeras.

7. Se casó con Isabel Preysler el 20 de enero de 1971 y tuvieron tres hijos: Chabely, Julio José y Enrique. El matrimonio terminó en 1979.

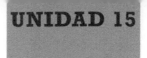

3 ¡Al borde de un ataque de nervios! (On the verge of a nervous breakdown)

Practising your writing skills

You have been asked by a local magazine to write a short biography of Pedro Almodóvar, the Spanish film director. Use the information below and write Almodóvar's biography.

1951: Nacer en Calzada de Calatrava, (Provincia de Ciudad Real, España).

1960: Trasladarse a Madrigalejo con su familia. Empezar sus estudios en el Colegio de los Salesianos.

1968: Ir a Madrid. Empezar a trabajar en la Compañía Telefónica.

1977-88: Conocer artistas importantes de la "Movida Madrileña".

1980: Terminar su trabajo en la Telefónica.

1987: Tener su primer éxito comercial con la película *¿Qué he hecho yo para merecer ésto?*

1990: Ganar el Premio Goya con su película *Mujeres al borde de un ataque de nervios.*

4 ¿Cuánto tiempo?

Revising your grammar

Transform the sentences like the example.

Example: Hace tres años que trabajo en esta empresa.
Llevo tres años trabajando en esta empresa.

1 Hace media hora que espero el autobús.
....

2 ....
Llevo diez años viviendo en Madrid.

3 Hace tres meses que estudio español.
....

4 ....
Llevo siete años haciendo natación.

5 Hace tres años que juego al fútbol.
....

6 ....
Llevo una semana leyendo este libro.

5 Cuéntame

Practising your dialogue skills

a Write the questions for these answers.

Example: ¿Dónde naciste? Nací en Juárez, en 1960.

1 ....
Estudié en el colegio los Rosales.

2 ....
Viví en Acapulco tres años.

3 ....
Conocí a mi primer esposo en la Riviera Francesa.

4 ....
Nos casamos en 1983.

5 ....
Hace dos años que vivo en La Habana.

6 ....
Hago gimnasia todos los días.

7 ....
Llevo seis años casada.

b Now ask the same questions using the formal register, *usted*.

6 Un poco más

Revising your vocabulary

Complete the sentences with appropriate words.

1 Mi marido y yo .... en 1980.

2 Mi amiga Lucía .... en Florida el año pasado.

3 No me gusta .... de compras.

4 Me levanto a .... ocho.

5 Ayer mis amigos y yo .... al cine y .... una película cubana que .... llama *Fresas y Chocolate.*

6 El poeta Ruben Darío .... en 1867 y .... en 1916.

UNIDAD 16

Objectives

Booking a table in a restaurant
Understanding a menu

1 Restaurantes

Practising your reading skills

a Here is a selection of some of Madrid's restaurants. Match the appropriate advertisement with the information below. Where would you choose to go if you wanted the following:

1 Celebrar una comida de negocios. ☐

2 Un restaurante cerca del hotel. Estás en el Hotel Plaza. ☐

3 No quieres comer carne ni pescado. ☐

4 Cenar muy tarde, después de las doce de la noche. ☐

5 Comer mariscos y pescado. ☐

6 Escuchar música mexicana y comer tacos. ☐

7 Ir a un restaurante uruguayo. ☐

8 Cocina española tradicional, especialmente jamón ibérico. ☐

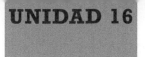

2 Reservar una mesa en un restaurante por teléfono

Practising your dialogue skills

Choose one of the restaurants from Activity 1 and book a table for two, for Saturday at 9.30 p.m.

R: **Dígame.**

Tú: ¿ .... ?

R: **Sí, aquí el restaurante ....**

Tú: ....

R: **¿A nombre de quién?**

Tú: ....

R: **¿Para que día?**

Tú: ....

R: **¿Para cuántas personas?**

Tú: ....

R: **¿Para qué hora quiere la mesa?**

Tú: ....

R: **Muy bien, tiene la mesa reservada para el sábado a las nueve y media.**

Tú: ....

R: **De nada. Adiós.**

Tú: ....

Tarta de queso
Chuletas de cerdo con patatas
Espinacas a la catalana
Sopa de pescado
Macedonia de frutas
Flan con nata
Cóctel de gambas
Trucha a la navarra
Huevos con jamón
Cordero asado
Espárragos con mayonesa
Helado

3 El menú

Test your knowledge of Spanish food

a The dishes listed below on the left for this restaurant menu are mixed up. Can you group and write them in the right sections? (A clue: Hay cuatro primeros; cuatro segundos y cuatro postres.)

b Now complete the following dialogue, ordering your favourite dishes from the menu.

Camarero: **¿Qué va a tomar?**

Tú: ....

Camarero: **¿Y de segundo?**

Tú: ....

Camarero: **¿Y para beber?**

Tú: ....

Camarero: **¿Tomará postre?**

Tú: ....

Primero
....
....
....
....

Segundo
....
....
....
....

Postre
....
....
....
....

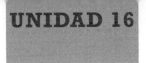

4 A/ de/ con/ para

Practising prepositions

In this dialogue there are some mistakes.
Can you correct them using the appropriate
preposition?

A: ¿Qué van tomar?

....

B: Yo, primero sopa con ajo, y de segundo un
filete a la plancha de ensalada.

....

C: Y, por mí, guisantes con jamón y pollo al ajillo.

....

A: ¿Y por beber?

....

B: Agua mineral a gas.

....

A: ¿Qué van a tomar a postre?

....

B: Flan de nata y macedonia con frutas.

....

5 Superlatives

Substitute the expressions in brackets
using the superlative form.

Example: El vino está (muy bueno) buenísimo.

1 Manolo es (muy alto) ....

2 Ayer estuvimos en un restaurante (muy caro)

....

3 Las gambas estaban (muy ricas) ....

4 La conferencia fue (muy interesante)

....

5 Las espinacas están (muy buenas)

....

6 El domingo estuvimos en una fiesta (muy
aburrida) ....

7 El examen fue (muy difícil) ....

6 Ocio

Practising your reading skills

a Read the article and mark if the following
statements are true or false.

1 Los españoles prefieren estar con los amigos
en bares, restaurantes y discotecas. ☐

2 En España hay más bares y restaurantes que
en toda Europa. ☐

3 Los españoles estamos con los amigos tres
horas al día. ☐

4 Los hombres de negocios se citan en
restaurantes. ☐

5 El 53% de los españoles practica un
deporte. ☐

Los españoles y el tiempo libre

Los españoles gastamos mucho en los bares.

Según el Centro de Investigaciones sobre Realidad Social, las actividades favoritas de los españoles son: relacionarnos con los demás, practicar deporte y ver la televisión. Para disfrutar con los amigos preferimos los restaurantes, bares y discotecas y en ello gastamos el 11% del consumo privado. Según datos del Instituto Nacional de Estadística, en España hay cerca de 230.000 bares y restaurantes, más que la suma total de toda Europa. Los españoles y los suecos somos los europeos que más tiempo dedicamos a estar con los amigos: dos horas y media al día.

Los bares y los restaurantes son los establecimientos de la sociabilidad. No vamos a una cafetería sólo a tomar una copa, también a estar con los demás. Las parejas se citan en los bares, los hombres de negocios en los restaurantes ... En relación al deporte, el 35% de la población lo practica de manera regular.

Vocabulary
Según: according to
consumo privado: private consumption
citarse: to meet

24

b Now write a paragraph about what people in
your country spend their leisure time doing.

UNIDAD 17

Objectives

Giving instructions
Giving formal and informal commands
Describing people's appearance: clothes

1 El robot multi-uso

Practising the imperative form

Robotberto is a robot specially designed to help you with the housework. It will do anything you want as long as you use the appropriate commands: the informal imperative form. Here is the list of things you want Robotberto to do. Use the appropriate command!

Barrer el suelo ....
Lavar la ropa ....
Hacer la comida ....
Limpiar las ventanas ....
Planchar ....
Regar las plantas ....
Hacer la compra ....
Llevar a los niños al parque ....
Ir a la farmacia y comprar aspirinas ....

2 En la consulta del médico

Practising your dialogue skills: the formal imperative

Complete the dialogue with the appropriate instructions. Use the pictures as cues.

Médico: [1]..................... **por favor.**

Paciente: **Hola, buenos días.**

Médico: [2]..
Vamos a ver, ¿qué le ocurre?

Paciente: **Pues me** [2a].................. **mucho este brazo.**

Médico: **Voy a examinarlo. Por favor,** [3].................. **ahí en la camilla.** [4].......................... **el brazo un poco. Así, muy bien. ¿**[4a]..................... **duele?**

Paciente: **¡Mucho!**

Médico: [5]..................... **, si es tan amable. No es nada importante.**

Un músculo un poco inflamado. [6]........................... **estas pastillas y** [6a]... **esta pomada tres veces al día.**

[7].............................. **dentro de una semana para ver que tal se encuentra.**

Hoy, 10 enero   17 enero

Paciente: **Muchas gracias. Hasta la semana que viene.**

Médico: **Adiós. Que se mejore.**

3 El robot perdido

Giving directions

Robotberto went shopping and got lost. Can you help him to find his way home? Remember that Robotberto only understands the informal imperative form.

4 La ropa

Revising your vocabulary

Write the names of these items.

5 ¿Tú qué piensas?

Giving advice about clothes

These people are not sure what clothes to wear. Can you give them some suggestions as in the example?

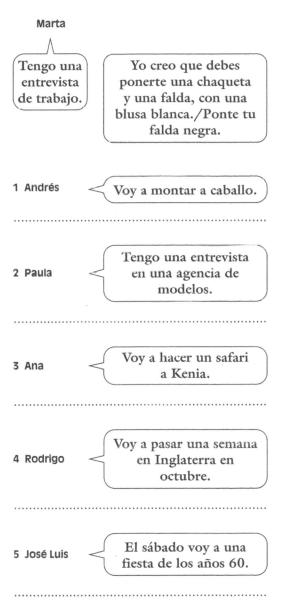

Marta

Tengo una entrevista de trabajo.

Yo creo que debes ponerte una chaqueta y una falda, con una blusa blanca./Ponte tu falda negra.

1 Andrés — Voy a montar a caballo.

....

2 Paula — Tengo una entrevista en una agencia de modelos.

....

3 Ana — Voy a hacer un safari a Kenia.

....

4 Rodrigo — Voy a pasar una semana en Inglaterra en octubre.

....

5 José Luis — El sábado voy a una fiesta de los años 60.

....

6 Soñando despiertos

Talking about dreams and ambitions

a Look at what these people say and guess what their dreams are.

> *Example:* **Martín: 'No tengo mucho dinero.'**
> **A Martín le gustaría tener más dinero.**

1 **Julia: 'Mi casa es muy pequeña.'**

....

2 **Carla: 'No toco muy bien la trompeta.'**

....

3 **Andrés: 'Sólo tengo dos semanas de vacaciones.'**.................................

4 **Eva: 'No tengo bastante tiempo para leer.'**

....

5 **Gabriel: 'Mi coche es muy viejo.'**

....

6 **Angeles: 'Trabajo demasiado.'**

....

b Ahora tú. What are your dreams and ambitions?

7 Un diseñador español

Practising your reading skills

Roberto Verino is one of the most successful fashion designers in Spain. He was interviewed by *El País* and below is an extract of that interview. Read it and decide whether these sentences are true or false.

1 **Roberto Verino no terminó sus estudios de arte.** ☐

2 **Nació en la ciudad de Orense.** ☐

3 **Piensa que el trabajo de un diseñador es vender magia.** ☐

4 **Roberto Verino piensa que no existe espíritu de competición entre los diseñadores.** ☐

5 **No le gusta que su ropa sea comercial.** ☐

6 **Admira a las españolas porque han evolucionado mucho en los últimos años.** ☐

7 **Le gustaría diseñar ropa para hombre pero no tiene tiempo.** ☐

8 **Su diseñador favorito es Armani.** ☐

ROBERTO VERINO ... DISEÑADOR
"No despego los pies del suelo"

R.G., Madrid

Abandonó sus estudios de arte en Paris para hacerse cargo de un negocio familiar de confección en su pueblo nata, Verín (Orense). Desde que en 1982 presentó su primera colección, Roberto Verino, cuyo verdadero nombre es Manuel Roberto Veriño, se ha convertido en el más claro ejemplo dentro del panorama de la moda española del equilibrio perfecto entre el diseño, la industria y la distribución. Verino afirma que la clave es la combinación del sueño y la realidad. "No despego los pies del suelo, pero para llegar lejos hay que soñar".

Pregunta. ¿Qué se vende en una pasarela?

Respuesta. Magia. Todo aquello que tiene que rodear a la moda para conseguir que esté por encima del realismo del día a día.

P. ¿Existe rivalidad entre los diseñadores?

R. Creo que sí. Siempre hay un criterio de estar atento y de tener un cierto interés para superarse a uno mismo y a los demás.

P. ¿Dónde está la frontera entre el diseño y la industria?

R. No hay una frontera estricta porque entiendo que el diseño puede ser industrial.

P. Algunos le tachan de ser excesivamente comercial.

R. Es verdad, pero estoy satisfecho con ese adjetivo.

P. ¿Cúal es su mujer ideal?

R. Para mí, la mujer ideal es la de este país que ha sido capaz de dar ese cambio tan importante desde el punto de vista social y de su propia actividad.

P. ¿Ha pensado alguna vez diseñar ropa de hombre?

R. Sí y la verdad me apetecería mucho hacerlo porque es para mí una alternativa más en la que me sentiría muy realizado. Lo que ocurre es que estoy tan involucrado en todos los proyectos que me falta el tiempo necesario para hacerlo bien.

P. Dígame un nombre del panorama internacional.

R. Siempre he sido un enamorado del trabajo de Giorgio Armani, al que considero un gran maestro.

P. ¿Quién es el juez de la moda?

R. Sin ninguna duda, la calle.

EL PAÍS

8 *La moda y tú*

Expressing your opinions and preferences about fashion

Write a short paragraph answering these questions.

1 ¿Te interesa la moda? ¿Por qué?

2 ¿Puedes definir tu estilo de vestir?

3 ¿Tienes ropa de diseño?

4 ¿Dónde compras normalmente la ropa? ¿Por qué?

5 ¿Te gustaría tener un estilo diferente?

6 ¿Qué opinas de los diseñadores de tu país? ¿Cuál es tu favorito?

9 *¿Qué haces tú para aprender un idioma?*

a Learning a language needs some time and also some learning strategies to learn more efficiently. Look at the list below and classify the activities from one to ten: 1 the most important, 10 the least important.

- **Estudiar gramática** ☐
- **Escuchar cintas** ☐
- **Leer periódicos y libros** ☐
- **Hacer ejercicios** ☐
- **Escribir** ☐
- **Estudiar un poco cada día y revisar mucho** ☐
- **Intentar no traducir literalmente** ☐
- **Hacer listas o diagramas de vocabulario alrededor de tópicos** ☐
- **Tener amigos de ese país y practicar con ellos** ☐
- **Deducir el significado de palabras nuevas por el contexto en el que están antes de mirar el diccionario** ☐

b Now write the *Perfect Student Decalogue* according to your classification in Activity a). Don't forget to follow it!

Example: **Haz ejercicios.**

Diseñador: Roberto Verino

Diseñador: Roberto Verino

UNIDAD 18

Objectives

Talking about plans and inviting
Buying clothes

1 La cartelera

Practising your reading skills

You are staying in Madrid with some friends and would like to invite them to go out during the weekend. You are looking at the *Guía del Ocio* to see what is on.

a Match the following words with the correct advert.

1 una obra de teatro □
2 un restaurante □
3 un concierto de música clásica □
4 una exposición □
5 una película □
6 un recital de flamenco □
7 una discoteca □

b Read *La cartelera* again and mark whether the statements are True or False.

1 Es posible visitar la exposición de Mompó hasta finales de octubre. □

2 En la discoteca Atocha 38 hay salsa los sábados. □

3 La Vaca Argentina abre todos los días. □

4 El recital de flamenco empieza a las 23.00. □

5 El concierto de música clásica es el viernes solamente. □

c Can you answer the following questions?

1 ¿Qué película ponen en el cine Novedades?
....

2 ¿A qué hora cierra la discoteca Atocha 38?
....

3 ¿Cómo se llama una persona que canta flamenco?
....

4 ¿Cúanto cuestan las entradas de sala sinfónica el domingo?
....

LA CARTELERA

□ **Salvador Navarro, trompa. Orquesta**
[A] **Nacional de España. Dir.: Walter Weller.** Obras de R. Strauss y Beethoven. Auditorio Nacional de Música, sala sinfónica. Viernes y sábado, 19.30h.; domingo, 11.30h. Precio: entre 9 y 25€ (viernes y sábado); entre 7 y 13€ (domingos)

□ **Circulo de Bellas Artes.** Marqués de
[B] Casa Riera, 1. Tel. 91 531 77 00. Metro Banco de España.
VI Muestra Alternativa de Teatro Invierno de luna alegre. Teatro Yeses. Del 14 al 16 de octubre. 20h.

□ **Centro de Arte Afinsa.** Almirante, 5.
[C] 1° Izda. Tel. 91 532 74 74. Metro Colón. Mompó (pintura, obra gráfica y dibujos sobre papel). *Hasta finales de octubre.*

□ **Novedades.** Orense, 26. Metro
[D] Nuevos Ministerios.
8,50€. Miér. no fest. día del espectador, 7€
SALA 1. (Aforo: 507)
Hable con ella (16.15, 19.15 y 22.15 h.)

□ **PEÑA FOSFORITO.** Picos de Europa,
[E] 11 (Puente Vallecas). Sábado 11: actuación del cantaor flamenco **Rancapino** a las 23.30h.

□ **LA VACA ARGENTINA.** P° Pintor
[F] Rosales, 52 (Argüelles) tel.91 559 66 05. Coc. Argentina. Esp. Carnes estilo argentino. No cierra ningún día **(2)**

□ **ATOCHA 38.** Atocha, 38 (Antón Martín).
[G] Tel. 91 369 38 81. Tardes música joven: máquina house. Jueves, viernes y sábados noche salsa, ritmos calientes. Música en vivo. Efectos láser. Abierto sólo vier. sáb. y visperas. Hasta la 4 madrugada.

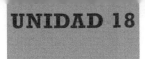

2 ¿Salimos esta noche?

Practising your dialogue skills

Choose what you want to do from Activity 1. Phone your friends Rosa and Juan and invite them to go out one evening over the weekend.

Tú: Hola, ¿ .... ?

Rosa: Sí, soy yo. Hola, ¿qué tal?

Tú: .... ¿Y .... ?

Rosa: Bien también.

Tú: ¿ .... ?

Rosa: Vamos al cine con mis padres.

Tú: ¡Qué lástima!

Tú: ¿Queréis .... el sábado, entonces?

Rosa: Sí, vale. De acuerdo.

Tú: ¿ .... ?

Rosa: A las 9 y media.

Tú: ¿ .... ?

Rosa: En la puerta del restaurante.

Tú: ....

Rosa: Hasta el sábado.

3 Vocabulario

Revising your vocabulary

a Look at these groups of words and spot the odd-one-out.

1 rayas   lunares   malva   cuadros   flores
2 lino   seda   lana   amarillo   algodón
3 vestido   chaqueta   rosa   calcetines   corbata
4 verde   rojo   azul   zapato   gris
5 grande   pequeño   oro   estrecho   corto

b Use the initials of the odd words and you will find the name of a month.

_ _ _ _ _

c Classify the words in Activity a) into these four groups: clothes, material, colour, pattern.

Ropa	Material	Color	Dibujo

4 De compras

Agreement of adjectives

How would you ask for the following items in a Spanish shop?

Example: **a pair of black trousers**
    Quisiera unos pantalones negros.
        a black T-shirt
    ¿Podría enseñarme una camiseta negra?

1 **a pair of brown leather shoes**

....

2 **a red and white striped cotton T-shirt**

....

3 **a pair of grey cotton trousers**

....

4 **a pink linen shirt**

....

5 **a pink wool pullover**

....

6 **a pair of white socks**

....

7 **a green silk shirt**

....

8 **a pair of green cotton shorts**

....

5 *Can I try it on?*

Direct object pronouns

Substitute the item using the direct object pronouns *lo*, *la*, *los*, *las*. Think about collocation and word order.

Example: **¿Puedo probarme la chaqueta azul?**
¿Puedo probármela?

1 Quisiera probarme este vestido.

....

2 ¿Puedo probarme la camisa roja?

....

3 Me llevo los pantalones negros.

....

4 ¿Tienen la corbata en otros colores?

....

5 Me llevo las camisetas roja y verde.

....

6 ¿Puedo probarme estos zapatos?

....

7 Me llevo la camisa de seda.

....

6 *En la tienda de ropa*

Practising your dialogue skills

You are in a shop with a friend and want to buy a pair of black trousers.

Dependiente: **¡Buenos días! ¿Qué desea?**

Tú: **Buenos días.** ....

Dependiente: **¿De que talla?**

Tú: ....

Dependiente: **Lo siento, pero negros no me quedan.**

Tú: ¿ .... ?

Dependiente: **De estas tallas, los tenemos en azul marino y en gris oscuro.**

Tú: ¿ ....?

Dependiente: **Sí, claro. Aquí los tiene.**

Tú: ¿ .... ?

Dependiente: **Los probadores están al fondo a la derecha.**

Tú: ¿ .... ?

Tu amigo/a: **Te quedan muy bien. Cómpratelos.**

Tú: ¿ .... ?

Dependiente: **Son 85 euros.**

Tú: **Vale,** ....

7 *Feria de Artesanía*

Read the advert and answer the questions below.

1 ¿Cuándo se celebra la Feria?

....

2 ¿En qué ciudad?

....

3 ¿Cuántos artesanos participan?

....

4 Menciona tres especialidades representadas en la Feria.

....

5 ¿De qué paises son los artesanos que exponen en la Feria?

....

6 ¿Los expositores representan a grandes o pequeñas empresas?

....

FERIAS

Expoarte
4–8 de diciembre.
Polígono Aeropuerto
Sevilla-Este. Sevilla.
Tel: (95) 467 51 40.
Fax: 467 53 50.

Artesanos de toda España y de varios países de Suramérica presentan su producción anual en la decimo-quinta edición de Expoarte. La feria andaluza es un amplísimo muestrario de los trabajos de artesanía o manufacturados de pequeñas empresas, que son distribuidos en una gran cantidad de comercios especializados. En más de cinco mil metros cuadrados expositivos, doscientos productores muestran sus realizaciones en cerámica, joyería, alfarería, confección de tejidos, fabricación de alfombras, marroquinería, piel y artículos de regalo.

Expoarte es una feria abierta a los diseñadores, artistas y fabricantes de países suramericanos. Treinta expositores de Bolivia, Perú, Argentina y Ecuador ofrecen en Sevilla lo mejor de su producción. Tejidos artesanos de Bolivia, cerámica y alfarería de Perú, trabajos en piel de Argentina y joyería de Ecuador pueden admirarse en este salón que une el arte con la producción industrial a pequeña escala.

8 ¿Refleja la ropa que llevas tu personalidad?

Test your reading and comprehension skills

Do the test and find out if your clothes reflect your personality!

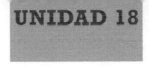

16

La ropa y tú

1 ¿Qué importancia tiene la ropa en tu vida?
- ❏ *a* Bastante.
- ❏ *b* Mucha.
- ❏ *c* Poca.

2 ¿Qué colores llevas normalmente?
- ❏ *a* Colores claros y suaves durante el día y oscuros por la noche.
- ❏ *b* Colores fuertes como rojo, naranja.
- ❏ *c* De todo un poco.

3 Cuándo vas a una fiesta,
- ❏ *a* te pones ropa elegante pero sofisticada.
- ❏ *b* llevas un modelo espectacular y original.
- ❏ *c* no me pongo nada especial.

4 ¿Qué tipo de ropa llevas normalmente?
- ❏ *a* Clásica y elegante.
- ❏ *b* Llamativa y divertida.
- ❏ *c* Cómoda.

5 ¿Te gustaría tener ropa de
- ❏ *a* Chanel o Hermés?
- ❏ *b* Jean Paul Gaultier?
- ❏ *c* Emporio Armani?

6 ¿Cuánto dinero gastas al mes en ropa?
- ❏ *a* Mucho.
- ❏ *b* Demasiado.
- ❏ *o* Poco.

7 Cuándo vas a comprar ropa,
- ❏ *a* eliges ropa clásica y de buena calidad que dure mucho tiempo.
- ❏ *b* siempre compras ropa de última moda.
- ❏ *c* normalmente compras vaqueros y camisetas.

Resultados

Cuenta las veces que has contestado **a**, **b** y **c** y lee después el resultado que has obtenido.

Mayoría de a: Eres una persona elegante que sabe vestirse apropiadamente para cada situación. Tu imagen es importante para tí. Prefieres tener poca ropa pero de buena calidad. Gastas bastante dinero pero sueles utilizar la ropa más de una temporada. Los díctámenes de la moda no te afectan mucho.

Mayoría de b: No puedes negar que eres una persona atrevida. Vas siempre a la última moda y no te importa llamar la atención. Eres una persona muy segura de tí misma. Te gastas demasiado dinero en ropa porque sueles utilizarla sólo una temporada.

Mayoría de c: Eres una persona muy práctica. Lo más importante para tí es la comodidad. No te gastas mucho dinero en ropa porque no lo consideras necesario.

Objectives

Saying what you have done
Reporting lost or stolen things
Describing people's appearance
in the past

1 Un recorrido turístico

Contrasting past and future tenses

Gabriela and Margarita are visiting Buenos Aires. Look at the list of things they want to do and say what things they have already done and what they are going to do next.

Example: **Han visitado la Casa Rosada. Van a comprar un billete para Iguazú.**

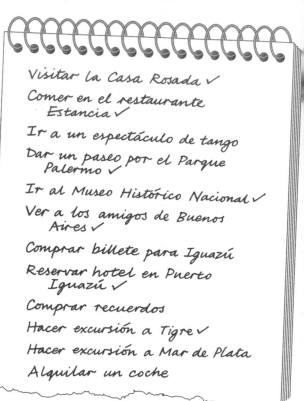

Visitar la Casa Rosada ✓
Comer en el restaurante Estancia ✓
Ir a un espectáculo de tango
Dar un paseo por el Parque Palermo ✓
Ir al Museo Histórico Nacional ✓
Ver a los amigos de Buenos Aires ✓
Comprar billete para Iguazú
Reservar hotel en Puerto Iguazú ✓
Comprar recuerdos
Hacer excursión a Tigre ✓
Hacer excursión a Mar de Plata
Alquilar un coche

....
....
....
....
....
....
....
....
....

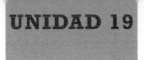
2 ¡Pero qué niño!

Practice of question forms with the pretérito perfecto (present perfect)

a Marquitos is a cute five-year-old boy but he is also very inquisitive. Can you write the questions he is asking his mum?

Example: **1 Oye, mamá, ¿has estado en la luna?**

1
¿estar en la luna?

2
¿subir al Himalaya?

3
¿ver un ovni?

4
¿comer pulpo?

5
¿ver un fantasma?

6
¿montar en camello?

7
¿emborracharse?

8
¿enamorarse?

1	5 ....
2	6 ....
3	7 ....
4	8 ....

b Now it is your turn to answer Marquitos' questions. Have you ever done those things?

3 En el trabajo

Practising the contrast between ya/todavía

a While his boss was out, Pepe was in charge of doing certain jobs. Look at his list and complete the dialogue with the appropriate word.

ya   todavia/aún   todavia no/aún no

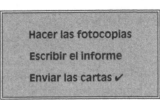

Hacer las fotocopias

Escribir el informe

Enviar las cartas ✔

Jefe: **Pepe, ... he vuelto. ¿Qué tal esos trabajillos? ¿Los ha terminado usted .... ?**

Pepe: **Pues, más o menos.**

Jefe: **Vamos a ver. ¿Ha hecho usted .... las fotocopias?**

Pepe: **..................................... Pero dentro de cinco minutos están preparadas.**

Jefe: **¿Y ha escrito el informe?**

Pepe: **No del todo. .... tengo que escribirlo a máquina. Pero .... he envíado las cartas.**

Jefe: **Muy bien. ¿Y qué más ha hecho?**

Pepe: **Pues, la verdad es que, nada más. Pero no se preocupe que .... tengo tres horas para terminarlo todo.**

b Ahora tú. Can you think of four things you have done today and three things that you still have to do? Write a list.

....
....
....
....
....
....
....

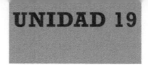

4 Los pronombres (pronouns)

Answer these questions as in the example. Don't forget that the pronouns change according to the gender of the subsistuted noun: *la, lo, las, los*.

Example: ¿Has hecho la cama hoy?
Sí, ya la he hecho./ No, no la he hecho todavía. Pero voy a hacerla más tarde.

1 ¿Has hecho la cama hoy?

....

2 ¿Has escuchado las noticias hoy?

....

3 ¿Has leído el periódico hoy?

....

4 ¿Has terminado tus ejercicios de español?

....

5 ¿Has limpiado la casa esta semana?

....

6 ¿Has visitado a tus amigos esta semana?

....

7 ¿Has tomado el metro hoy para ir a trabajar?

....

8 ¿Has pagado la renta este mes?

....

5 ¡Vaya Día de San Valentín!

Practising past participles and vocabulary

Today is Saint Valentine's Day and Emilio is waiting for his girlfriend, at the Cafetería La Mallorquina. Complete the dialogue using the past participles of the verbs in the box.

poner	romper	robar
tener	perder	pasar
poder	llegar	ir
ser	dar	

Águeda: Perdona por llegar tarde pero es no puedes imaginarte el día tan horrible que he ....

Emilio: Bueno, mujer. Tranquilízate y tómate algo. A ver, ¿qué te ha .... ?

Águeda: Primero, esta mañana he .... el tren y he .... tarde al trabajo. Después no he .... comer porque me dolían mucho las muelas. Luego se me ha .... el tacón del zapato y, para terminar, ¡me han .... el bolso!

Emilio: ¡No me digas! ¿Y cómo ha
.... ?

Águeda: Pues salía yo de Almacenes Arias, los de la calle Fuencisla, y me han .... el tirón.

Emilio: ¿Y llevabas mucho dinero encima?

Águeda: Pues en metálico no mucho, unas 50 euros. Pero llevaba todas mis tarjetas de crédito, las llaves de casa y del coche, el permiso de conducir, mi agenda roja ... En definitiva, todo. Incluído mi mejor bolso, el de piel marrón.

Emilio: ¿Y vas a poner una denuncia?

Águeda: Ya la he .... También he .... al banco para que anulen mis tarjetas... Lo peor es que también robaron tu regalo de San Valentín.

Emilio: ¡Vaya día de San Valentín!

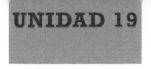
6 *En la compañía de seguros*

Writing a report for an insurance company

Águeda went to her insurance company and informed them about the incident. Complete the form with the information from Activity 5.

A

7 *Un informe para la policía*

Writing skills: describing people's appearance

After informing the insurance company, Águeda went to the police station to describe the suspects. How did she describe them?

SEGUROS LA EQUITATIVA S.A.

Póliza de asegurado
34164193

1 | Datos del asegurado

Apellidos | S a n t o s | M a n z a n o

Nombre

Domicilio | C / | B u i t r a g o | 1 6 | 3 ° A

Código postal | 2 9 0 1 3 | Teléfono | 6 3 1 9 6 5 0

2 | Declaración de daños

(Marque con una cruz [X] el recuadro apropiado)

a

Pérdida [ ]   Accidente [ ]

Avería [ ]   Robo [ ]

b

Fecha del suceso

Lugar del suceso

En caso de robo, ¿ha presentado usted denuncia a la policía?

Sí [ ]   No [ ]

c

Descripción de objeto y contenido

Firma *Águeda Santos Manzano*

Uno de los ladrones era alto ....
....
....
....
....
....
....
....
....
....
....

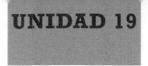

8 La importancia del español en el mundo

Developing your reading skills

a ¿Tú qué opinas?

1 **¿Cuál es el idioma extranjero que más se estudia en el Reino Unido?**

....

2 **En tu opinión, ¿para qué estudian español los británicos?**

....

3 **¿Por qué estudias tú español?**

....

b Read the text and check your answers.

C Read the text again and answer the questions below.

1 **¿Por qué ahora hay más estudiantes de español que antes?**

....

2 **¿Con qué problemas se encuentra la enseñanza del español en la escuela secundaria?** ....

3 **¿Qué ventajas tiene el español para los estudiantes?** ....

4 **¿Por qué en Irlanda del Norte y en Escocia el español es la segunda lengua más estudiada en la escuela secundaria?**

....

La importancia económica de España y Latinoamérica aumenta la demanda del idioma

Los ingleses, por aquello de que en todo el mundo se conoce su idioma, son los ciudadanos europeos con menor interés por aprender una segunda lengua. Hasta ahora. La creciente importancia de Latinoamérica y el empuje de instituciones hispanas han hecho que, en la última década, el número de estudiantes de español esté en aumento.

Según un estudio realizado por la Consejería de Educación de la Embajada Española en Londres, "el español está en clara progresión en la mayor parte de los sectores y centros de enseñanza británicos". El mayor interés se ha detectado en la enseñanza universitaria, donde el castellano alcanza un porcentaje del 24%

sobre la cifra total de estudiantes de lenguas extranjeras.

Actualmente, el francés ocupa la preferencia de los británicos. Pero con la introducción de la reforma educativa británica en 1988, se potenció la diversificación de la enseñanza de idiomas extranjeros, aunque no es fácil introducir el español.

Para el consejero de Educación en la Embajada Española en Gran Bretaña, la falta de tradición y la inexistencia de profesores son los principales obstáculos en la enseñanza secundaria.

Sin embargo, el castellano "motiva a los estudiantes porque, al principio, se obtienen mejores resultados en la comunicación que con otros idiomas," afirma

el consejero.

El estudio realizado destaca que, en Irlanda del Norte, el español se ha convertido en la segunda lengua extranjera en la enseñanza secundaria. La mayor demanda de castellano en Irlanda del Norte – algo similar ocurre en Escocia – responde al "entusiasmo de los profesores de esas áreas".

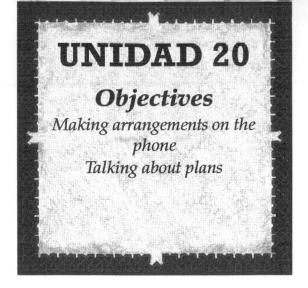

UNIDAD 20

Objectives

Making arrangements on the phone

Talking about plans

1 Revisión: vocabulario

Write the appropriate words and you will find the name of a very useful machine.

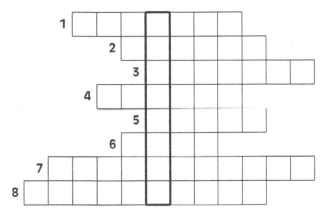

1 Me gusta llegar siempre a tiempo. Soy muy .....

2 ¿Cómo se dice *message* en español?

3 El sustantivo de llamar es .....

4 Sirve para anotar las cosas que tenemos que hacer.

5 ¿Está Lola, por .....?

6 Un momento, ahora se .....

7 No puedo hablar con ella, el teléfono está siempre .....

8 No, no es aquí. Se ha .....

2 Al teléfono

Making arrangements over the phone

Complete these telephone conversations as appropriate. Each gap may require one or more words.

1 A: ¿ .... Ana, por favor?

B: ¿ .... ?

A: De Manolo.

B: No, ...

A: ¿Sabe cuándo .... ?

B: A la hora de comer.

A: Vale, ... llame.

2 A: ¿ .... Arturo?

B: Sí, ... pone.

A: Hola Arturo, ... Paloma.

C: Hola Paloma, ¿ .... ?

A: Muy bien. ¿ .... ?

C: .... muy cansado. Tengo muchísimo trabajo.

A: ¿ .... a mi casa mañana por la noche?

C: Lo siento .... terminar un informe para el lunes.

A: Vale, ¡no trabajes demasiado!

C: Adiós y gracias.

A: ....

3 A: Seat, ¿ .... ?

B: .... ¿ .... con la Srta. Balduque?

A: ¿De parte de quién?

B: .... la Srta. López, de Fiat.

A: Un momento ... Lo siento, la Srta. Balduque .... reunión. ¿Quiere dejarle un recado?

B: Sí, dígale que he llamado y que .... a llamar más tarde.

A: Vale, adiós.

B: Adiós.

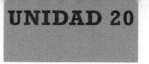

UNIDAD 20

3 ¿Quedamos el domingo?

This dialogue between two friends who want to go out on Sunday is mixed up. Read the dialogue and put it in the correct order.

B: Me gustaría ir a una exposición. ☐

A: ¿Dónde quedamos? ☐

A: ¿Qué podemos hacer el domingo? ☐

A: No, prefiero más tarde. ¿Te va bien a la 1.00? ☐

A: Vale, nos vemos a la una en la Puerta de Alcalá. ☐

A: Muy bien, hay una exposición muy interesante en El Retiro. ☐

B: ¿Quedamos a las 12.00? ☐

B: De acuerdo, entonces quedamos a la una. ☐

B: Podemos quedar en la puerta de Alcalá. ☐

4 Concertar una cita

Developing your dialogue skills

a Caroline works in London's Resaca Radio Sales department and she is going to Barcelona to see a colleague, Elena Puig, in Radio Candela. She needs to phone Barcelona and arrange an appointment with Elena. Complete the dialogue.

Recepcionista: **Radio Candela, ¿dígame?**

Caroline: ....

Recepcionista: **Buenos días.**

Caroline: .... **con la Srta. Puig del departamento de Ventas.**

Recepcionista: **¿De parte de quién?**

Caroline: .... **de Resaca Radio en Londres.**

Recepcionista: **Un momento, ahora le paso.**

Elena: **¿Dígame?**

Caroline: ...., **soy .... de Resaca Radio.**

Elena: **Hola, ¿qué tal?**

Caroline: **Bien, ¿ .... ?**

Elena: **Muy bien pero con mucho trabajo.**

Caroline: .... **a Barcelona la próxima semana y .... concertar una cita para hablar de los nuevos productos.**

Elena: **Un momento, voy a mirar mi agenda. El lunes y el martes estoy de viaje. ¿Te va bien el jueves por la mañana?**

Caroline: **Sí, ¿ .... ?**

Elena: **A las 10 o 10.30.**

Caroline: .... **10. ¿ .... ?**

Elena: **En mi oficina.**

Caroline: **Vale .... un fax, confirmando todos los detalles.**

Elena: **Muy bien. Hasta pronto.**

Caroline: ....

b Now write a fax with all the details about the trip.

Date of arrival 31st May 7.30 pm. Caroline will stay in Hotel Continental tel. 4159293, room 231 in case Elena needs to contact her. Confirm that Caroline will see Elena on Thursday 1st of June at 10.00 am in her office.

FAX

From: Resaca Radio London

To: Radio Candela Barcelona

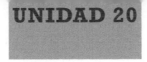
5 Horóscopo: ¿Qué signo eres?

Developing your reading skills

a Read your horoscope with a dictionary if necessary. See if it comes true.

 Aries 21 marzo – 20 abril

Deberás cuidar tus relaciones laborales para evitar problemas. Te encontrarás animado con el dinero y gastarás demasiado. En las relaciones personales se dará un gran dinamismo y desearás hacer unas fiestas con tus amigos.

 Tauro 21 abril – 20 mayo

Se cumplirán algunas de tus aspiraciones. Una cuestión económica te podrá preocupar, pero no te impedirá disfrutar. Será un período favorable para la amistad, las relaciones y las novedades.

 Géminis 21 mayo – 21 junio

Estarás sensible a los problemas con otras personas. Intentarás ayudar. Será un buen momento para la expresión y desarrollo de tus sentimientos. Tendrás buena suerte en asuntos de dinero o trabajo.

 Cáncer 22 junio – 22 julio

Habrá luna llena en tu signo. Encontrarás acontecimientos y novedades en tu trabajo. Harás un viaje interesante o importante. Te sentirás optimista para empezar u organizar cosas. Tus sentimientos estarán abiertos a la amistad.

 Leo 23 julio – 23 agosto

Estarás dinámico en tus actividades profesionales y tendrás que tomar una decisión difícil. Algún problema económico retrasará algo que deseas hacer. Te sentirás inclinado a buscar una velada íntima para sorprender a tu pareja.

 Virgo 24 agosto – 21 septiembre

Tus intereses profesionales tomarán un nuevo ritmo de acuerdo con tus aspiraciones. Te gustará el estado de tu cuenta bancaria y te hará sentirte bien. En las relaciones de pareja habrá pequeñas discusiones y problemas.

 Libra 22 septiembre – 22 octubre

Estarás muy animado por las novedades que están pasando estos días pero también nervioso por algunas situaciones difíciles. Realizarás un viaje con tu pareja.

 Escorpio 23 octubre – 21 noviembre

Será un período muy favorable en general y, sobre todo para las relaciones, los sentimientos y los hijos. Encontrarás satisfacción en tus actividades que te gustará. El tema económico marchará bien y podrá ser muy productivo.

 Sagitario 22 noviembre – 22 octubre

Estarás nervioso e inquieto, necesitas relajarte; reflexiona y trabaja sin prisas. Deberás tener cuidado con el dinero y no gastar demasiado porque las consecuencias serán negativas.

 Capricornio 23 diciembre – 21 enero

Ten cuidado con tu dinero y propiedades. Trabaja con calma y todo te irá bien. Una situación poco clara en las relaciones sentimentales te pondrá un poco nervioso y de mal humor.

 Acuario 22 enero – 19 de febrero

Tendrás que resolver una situación delicada en tu trabajo. Estarás de acuerdo con tu pareja en realizar una compra o inversión.

 Piscis 20 febrero – 20 marzo

En el terreno profesional y social será un período lleno de acontecimientos. Tendrás posibilidades de promoción o de mejoras económicas. Te sentirás de buen humor y estarás dispuesto para divertirte con tus amigos.

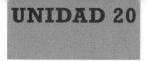

b These people have read their horoscope. Can you guess their star sign?

> Haré un viaje.

1 ....

> Haré una fiesta con mis amigos.

2 ....

> ¡Uff, tengo que tener cuidado con el dinero!

3 ....

> Según el horóscopo voy a tener una discusión con mi novio.

4 ....

> Voy a hacer un viaje con mi novia.

5 ....

c ¿Puedes imaginarte como serás dentro de diez años?

Example: **Viviré en una casa en el campo.**

6 Tarot

a Do you know The Tarot? What is your number? Follow the instructions and find out!

Add up the numbers of your birthday and reduce them to one digit.

Example: **6th October 1956: 6+10+1+9+5+6 = 37; 3+7 = 10; 1+0 = 1. Your number is 1.**

b Read what the Tarot predictions are for this week. Can you interpret the Tarot chart for some of your friends? Write a paragraph for each friend using the information in the chart. First of all you need to calculate their tarot number.

Example: **Number 2. Tendrán una situación muy favorable en el trabajo y en la salud. Las relaciones con su pareja y sus amigos serán buenas. En los juegos de azar, la semana se presentará buena. Su número de la suerte es el 18. No harán muchos viajes.**

	1	2	3	4	5	6	7	8	9
Trabajo	B	MB	MB	R	MB	B	B	R	B
Salud	B	MB	B	B	R	B	MB	R	B
Amor	B	B	B	B	R	MB	B	MB	MB
Azar	R	B	MB	B	R	MB	R	B	B
Amistad	MB	B	MB	MB	MB	MB	R	MB	B
Familia	B	MB	MB	B	MB	R	B	MB	B
Viajes	B	R	B	R	B	MB	B	R	MB
Dinero	B	B	MB	B	B	MB	B	R	MB
Sorpresas	F	F	F	F	F	F	F	F	F
N° suerte	33	18	45	94	12	71	88	4	2
Días fav.	19	20	16	19	20	17	19	14	17
Días desfav.	14	18	18	17	17	19	17	16	14
Arc. tarot	Cab copas	Dos oros	Sola oros	Siete oros	Diez copas	Nueve bastos	As oros	Seis bastos	Rey bastos

B = bien, D = desfavorable, E = excelente, F = favorable, M = mal, MB = muy bien, MF = muy favorable, R = regular

ANSWER KEY

UNIDAD 1

2 **a** Argentina/Chile/Gran Bretaña/
Japón/Alemania/Holanda/Portugal/España
b En Argentina y en Chile se habla
español./En Gran Bretaña se habla inglés, galés
y gaélico./En Japón se habla japonés./En
Alemania se habla alemán./En Holanda se habla
holandés./En Portugal se habla portugués./En
España se habla español, catalán, vasco y gallego.

3 Possible answers: **a** Me llamo (John).
b Sí, soy de Londres./No, soy de Manchester.
c Vivo en (Surrey). **d** Sí, hablo (francés) y un
poquito de (alemán)./ No, ninguna.

4 **Yo:** hablo, vivo, soy, me llamo **TU:** vives,
te llamas, eres, hablas **El/ella/usted:** se
llama, habla, es , vive

5 **a** ¿Cómo te llamas?/¿Cuál es tu nombre?
(LA)/¿De dónde eres?/¿Dónde vives?/¿Qué
lenguas/idiomas hablas?
b ¿Cómo se llama (usted)?/¿Cuál es su
nombre? (LA)/¿De dónde es (usted)?/¿Dónde
vive (usted)?/¿Qué lenguas habla?

6 Se llama Beatriz. Es de Rosario, Argentina,
pero vive en Madrid. Habla español y francés. Se
llama Pep y es de Barcelona, pero vive en
Londres. Habla catalán, inglés e italiano. Y
también habla español, claro.

7 **1** 9.00. Hola, buenos días. **2** 12.30.
hola, buenos días. **3** 14.30. Hola, buenas
tardes. **4** 18.45. Hola, buenas tardes.
5 22.15. Adiós, buenas noches.

8 **1** Marta Gómez Martínez **2** española
3 Montevideo, Uruguay. 10.4.56
4 Barcelona **5** 10 years

9 **1** hospital **2** teléfono **3** pasaporte
4 restaurante **5** bar **6** aeropuerto **7** hotel

UNIDAD 2

1 **a 1** médico **2** arquitecto **3** alemana
4 hermana **5** secretaria **6** enfermera
b Nacionalidad: inglés, francés,
canadiense, alemana, italiana, española, mexicana
Profesión: médico, arquitecto, pintor, actor,
profesor, secretaria, estudiante, enfermera,
carpintero **Familia:** padre, hija, tío, hermana,
madre, abuela, marido

2 **a** Esta es Carmen Herrera. Es española y
vive en Madrid. Es arquitecta y trabaja en la
empresa Proyectista Internacional.
b Este es Rodolfo Prados. Es
costarricense y vive en San José. Es ingeniero y
trabaja en la empresa Construcciones S.A.
Esta es Nicole Dubois. Es francesa y vive en
Nantes. Es profesora y trabaja en la Universidad
de Nantes./Esta es Rosa Oliveira. Es portuguesa
y vive en Lisboa. Es diseñadora y trabaja para/
en Ofimagen, S.L./Este es Roberto Manzoni.
Es italiano y vive en Milán. Es pintor y trabaja
en la Escuela de Arte de Milán.
c Soy (Martin Hume, etc.). Soy
(nationality: inglés/inglesa, etc.) y vivo en
(city/town you live in). Soy (= your job) y
trabajo en (la empresa X, un banco, etc.).

3 **a 1** *A:* Le/ a la *B:* Encantada
2 *A* Te/ a *C:* Hola
b Señor Lobos, le presento a la señora
Losada, de Argentina./Sergio, te presento a
Roberto./ Este es Roberto./Señora Arribas, le
presento al señor Peña, de Venezuela./Carlos, te
presento a Luisa./Esta es Luisa.

4 No, soy boliviana./Trabajo de recepcionista
pero estudio enfermería. Es mi vocación. ¿Y tú?
¿En qué trabajas?/Soy pintor pero trabajo de
intérprete./¿Cuántos idiomas hablas?/¿Dónde
vives?/¿Cuántos hijos tienes?/Yo también.

6 **a 1** Rafael es su tío. **2** Emilio es su
padre. **3** Mercedes es su madre. **4** Carmen
es su tía. **5** Manuel y Isabel son sus abuelos.
b 1 Beatriz: Lola, ésta es mi madre.
2 Beatriz: Este es mi padre. **3** Beatriz: Y éste
es mi hermano Arturo.

UNIDAD 3

1 **Una ciudad:** moderna, turística, bonita,
acogedora, ruidosa, alegre, grande **Un pueblo:**
pequeño, antiguo, tranquilo, acogedor, aburrido,
alegre, grande

2 **1** e **2** b **3** f **4** c **5** g **6** d **7** a

3 **a Horizontal words:** Line 1 teatro/
Line 2 parque/Line 5 mercado/Line 8 farmacia/
Line 11 hotel
Vertical words: Line 1 restaurante/Line 2
iglesia/Line 4 estanco/Line 7 bar, banco

b un mercado, un estanco, una farmacia,
un parque, una iglesia, un bar, un teatro, un
banco, un hotel, un restaurante
c unos mercados, unos estancos, unas
farmacias, unos parques, unas iglesias, unos
bares, unos teatros, unos bancos, unos hoteles,
unos restaurantes

4 **a 1** ¿Hay un estanco por aquí? **2** ¿Hay
una farmacia cerca de aquí? **3** ¿Me puede
decir si hay un hotel por aquí?
b 1 c **2** a **3** b

5 **1** ¿Hay un estanco por aquí? **2** ¿Hay una
oficina de Correos por aquí cerca? **3** ¿Hay una
panadería por aquí? **4** ¿Hay una tienda de
ropa por aquí? **5** ¿Hay una farmacia por aquí?
6 ¿Hay un bar por aquí? **7** ¿Hay un
restuarante cerca de aquí?

6 **a** Hay una en la Calle Descalzas **b** Hay
uno en la Calle Mayor y otro en la Plaza
Grande. **c** Hay uno en la Calle Feria.
d Hay una en la Avenida Donosti. **e** Hay
uno en la Calle de la Fe.

7 **1** tranquilo **2** hay **3** varias **4** en
5 bares **6** una **7** muy **8** antigua **9** el
10 un **11** de **12** muchos **13** pero
14 cerca

8 **1** Segovia. **2** Un Acueducto, el Alcázar,
la Plaza mayor y la Catedral. **3** El Acueducto.
4 Comer y beber (eating and drinking),
Comprar artesanía (buying crafts).

UNIDAD 4

1 **A:** Perdona, ¿hay un estanco por aquí?
B: Sí, hay uno en la calle Justicia, entre la tienda
de ropa y la farmacia. **A:** ¿Y puede decirme
(sabe) donde está el mercado? **B:** En la calle
Agustinos, enfrente de la lavandería.
A: ¿Puede decirme si hay (sabe si hay) un
restaurante barato? **B:** Hay uno en la calle
Ronda, a la izquierda, enfrente del bar.
A: Por último, ¿dónde puedo coger el autobús
29? Necesito ir al centro. **B:** Pues, al lado del
bar, en la misma calle Ronda. **A:** Muchas
gracias. **B:** De nada.

2 **1** Hay un bar enfrente del restaurante. **2** La farmacia está enfrente del hospital. **3** Hay una parada de autobús delante del bar. **4** Mi casa está a la izquierda. **5** El Museo arqueológico está en la calle Serrano. **6** ¿Me da un horario de autobuses? **7** Toledo está a 72 km. de Madrid.

3 **1** veinticinco (25) – cincuenta y dos (52) **2** sesenta y siete (67) – setenta y seis (76) **3** ochenta y seis (86) – sesenta y ocho (68) **4** catorce (14) – cuarenta y uno (41) **5** noventa y ocho (98) – ochenta y nueve (89) **6** cincuenta y seis (56) – sesenta y cinco (65)

4 **1** Es la tercera. **2** En el primero, puerta tercera. **3** Es la segunda a la derecha. **4** En el segundo piso, puerta quinta. **5** En el tercero, puerta cuarta. **6** Es el segundo.

5 **A:** ¿Tiene (Me puede dar)...?/¿Puede decirme (Sabe) cómo se va al ...?/**B:** ... final de esta calle .../**A:** ¿Está lejos?/¿Y hay (puede decirme si hay/ sabe si hay) un ...?/**A:** ¿Es caro?

6 **1** b **2** f **3** d **4** e **5** c **6** a

7 **a** Sigues todo recto, coges la primera calle a la izquierda y la tercera a la derecha. Sigues recto y coges la segunda calle a la izquierda y después la primera a la derecha. Coges la segunda calle a la derecha y después la primera a la izquierda. Sigues recto hasta el final de la calle, giras a la derecha, tomas la primera a la izquierda y otra vez la primera a la izquierda. Por último coges la primera calle a la derecha. La princesa esta allí esperándote.

8 **a** **Cádiz:** 4 **A Coruña:** 6 **Zaragoza:** 8

UNIDAD 5

1 **a** **Across:** **1** mantequilla **2** tomates **3** patatas **4** naranjas **5** arroz **6** vino **Down:** **1** galletas **2** queso **3** jamón **4** platanos **5** leche **6** pan

b **Una botella de:** vino **Un litro de:** leche **Una barra de:** pan **Una bolsa de:** patatas fritas **Un paquete de:** arroz, mantequilla, galletas **Un trozo de:** jamón, queso **Un kilo de:** tomates, naranjas, (jamón), (queso)

2 **1** Pescadería **2** Frutería **3** Panadería **4** Charcutería **5** Confitería ESTANCO

3 **Bebidas:** cava, cerveza, vino, ron, tequila **Carne:** pollo, chuletas de cerdo, conejo **Pescado:** sardinas, truchas, calamares, atún, gambas **Fruta:** mangos, aguacates, manzanas **Verdura:** judías verdes, cebollas, lechuga, tomates **Embutidos:** chorizo, salchichón, queso manchego

4 **1** ¿Cuántas manzanas quiere? **2** ¿Cuántos mangos quiere? **3** ¿Cuántas lechugas quiere? **4** ¿Cuánto es? **5** ¿Cuántas botellas de vino quiere?

5 100 – cien/458 – cuatrocientos cincuenta y ocho/1.879 – mil ochocientos setenta y nueve/567 – quinientos sesenta y siete/780 – setecientos ochenta/135 – ciento treinta y cinco/2.500 – dos mil quinientos/5.768 – cinco mil setecientos sesenta y ocho/6.690 – seis mil seiscientos noventa/14.975 – catorce mil novecientos setenta y cinco

6 (Notice that you do not need to use all the words in bracket. They are just different possibilities.) Buenos días./(Quería/Quiero/ Quisiera/Me da) una botella de vino tinto./Sí, (quería/ quisiera/ quiero/ me da) medio de kilo de queso./¿Tienen jamón? Me da cuarto de kilo de jamón serrano./Ah, quería también una bolsa de patatas grande./No, nada más. ¿Cuánto es?

7 **1** c **2** a **3** b

4 **1** nos levantamos **2** desayunamos **3** leemos **4** limpiamos **5** hacemos **6** tomamos **7** salimos **8** vamos **9** vamos **10** comemos **11** escuchamos **12** leemos **13** nos acostamos **14** vamos

5 Antonio barre a veces./ los lunes y los miércoles./ dos veces a la semana./Paco y Marta barren tres veces a la semana/ los martes, viernes y domingos./Antonio friega los platos tres veces a la semana./ los domingos, lunes y martes./Paco y Marta friegan los platos tres veces a la semana./ los martes, viernes y domingos./Antonio no lava la ropa nunca./ Antonio nunca lava la ropa./Paco y Marta lavan la ropa dos veces a la semana./ los jueves y sábados./Antonio plancha una vez a la semana./ los domingos./Paco y Marta planchan a veces./ dos veces a la semana./ los miércoles y sábados./Antonio saca la basura a veces./ dos días a la semana./ los lunes y viernes./ dos veces por semana./Paco y Marta sacan la basura cuatro veces a la semana./ todas las noches./ los martes, miércoles, jueves y domingos./Antonio nunca prepara la cena./ No prepara la cena nunca./Paco y Marta preparan la cena todos los días./ los lunes, martes, miércoles, jueves, viernes, sábados, domingos./ todas las noches.

6 **a** Fue escritora.
b **1** True **2** False **3** False **4** False **5** True **6** False

UNIDAD 7

1 **a** **1** b **2** e **3** a **4** c **5** d **6** f
b **1** Beatriz Sierra, Pº del Prado nº 59, 7º B, 28002 Madrid **2** Jose Luis Porta, C/ 29 esq. Pza. San Rafael, La Habana, Cuba **3** Francisco Mendoza, 32 Avda. 27-22, Zona 5, Ciudad de Guatemala, Guatemala

2 **a** alquilar un piso – 201/alquilar un apartamento – 205/alquilar un chalé – 203
b **1** habitación – hab. **2** ascensor – ascen./ asc. **3** calefacción – calef. **4** terraza – tza. **5** cocina nueva – cocina nva. **6** cocina equipada – coc. equip. **7** puerta blindada – pta. blind.

3 **a** Buenas tardes/¿Cómo es el piso?/ ¿Cuántas habitaciones tiene?/¿Todas las habitaciones son exteriores?/¿Tiene ascensor?/ ¿Tiene calefacción?/¿Tiene terraza?/¿dónde está?/¿Tiene aire acondicionado?

UNIDAD 6

1 **a** **1** desayunar **2** terminar **3** comer **4** salir **5** volver **6** empezar **7** acostarse **8** ir **9** cenar **10** levantarse
b **1** trabaja **2** se levanta **3** desayuna **4** Sale **5** Va **6** Empieza **7** va **8** come **9** termina **10** vuelve **11** cena **12** se acuesta.

2 **1** ¿Qué desayunas? **2** ¿A qué hora empiezas a trabajar? **3** ¿Cómo vas a trabajar? **4** ¿Con quién comes? **5** ¿A qué hora vuelves a casa? **6** ¿A qué hora te acuestas?

3 **1** ¿A qué hora vuelves a casa normalmente? **2** ¿Trabajas por la tarde? **3** ¿Vas a trabajar en autobús? **4** ¿A qué hora terminas de trabajar? **5** Normalmente salgo de casa muy temprano. **6** ¿A qué hora empiezas a trabajar? **7** ¿Trabajas en una oficina? **8** ¿A qué hora os acostáis?

74

b Advert : 3 dormitorios, todo exterior, tiene aire acondicionado   Actual flat: 2 dormitorios, el baño es interior, no tiene aire acondicionado

4 **1** es **2** es **3** está **4** es **5** es **6** está **7** es **8** está **9** está **10** es

5 **1** ¿Te gustan los gatos? Detesto/ No me gustan nada los gatos, pero me encantan/ me gustan mucho los perros. **2** ¿Te gusta la salsa? Sí, me gusta mucho/ me encanta. **3** ¿Te gusta la comida mexicana? Sí me encanta/ me gusta mucho. **4** ¿Te gusta la Opera? Detesto la Opera./ No me gusta nada la Opera, pero me encanta la música pop. **5** ¿Te gustan los pasteles? No me gustan nada./ Detesto los pasteles, pero me encanta/ me gusta mucho el chocolate.

6 Pilar: No me gustan los gatos. Pepe: A mí tampoco. Ana: A mí sí./Pilar: Me gusta la comida china. Pepe: A mí no. Ana: A mí sí./Pilar: Me gusta el español. Pepe: A mi también. Ana: A mi también./Pilar: Me gusta el tenis. Pepe: A mí no. Ana: A mí sí./Pilar: No me gusta la música rock. Pepe: A mí tampoco. Ana: A mí tampoco./Pilar: Me gustan los perros. Pepe: A mí también. Ana: A mí no.

7 **1** No me gustan nada los gatos. **2** A mi hermano le gusta jugar al fútbol. **3** ¿Os gusta la música clásica? **4** A mis padres les gusta la comida italiana. **5** A nosotros nos encanta bailar.

8 **a** Sí, porque a Buñuel le gusta comer temprano. **b** Sí, porque le gusta el ruido de la lluvia. **c** Sí, porque le gusta el frío. **d** No, porque no le gustan ni el desierto ni la arena. **e** No, porque le gusta la puntualidad. **f** No, porque le gustan los bares, el alcohol y el tabaco. **g** No, porque no le gustan las estadísticas. **h** No, porque no le gustan los banquetes. **i** No, porque detesta la proliferación de información.

UNIDAD 8

1 **1** ¿Cómo te llamas? **2** ¿A qué hora sale el tren? **3** ¿Dónde vives? **4** ¿Cuántos hermanos tiene? **5** ¿A qué distancia está Zaragoza de Madrid? **6** ¿Dónde te duele? **7** ¿Cuánto es todo? **8** ¿De dónde es Marina? **9** ¿Quién es esa Señora? Es mi madre. **10** ¿Cómo es tu hermana?

2 **a** 5 **b** 4 **c** 1 **d** 2 **e** 3 **f** 6

3 **1** alta – baja **2** simpáticos – antipáticos **3** feo – guapo **4** aburrida – divertida **5** viejo – joven **6** inteligentes – tontos/as **7** gordo – flaco/delgado **8** rubio – moreno **9** tímidas – extrovertidas

4 **a 1** Me duele la cabeza. **2** Me duele la barriga. **3** Me duelen las piernas. **4** Me duelen los ojos. **5** Estoy enfermo/a. **6** Tengo fiebre. **7** Tengo tos. **8** Estoy resfriado.
   b 1 Tienes que tomar una aspirina./ Debes tomar una aspirina. **2** Tienes que tomar manzanilla./ Debes tomar manzanilla. **3** Tienes que descansar./ Debes descansar. **4** Tienes que ir al oculista./ Debes ir al ... **5** Tienes que ir al médico./ Debes ir al ... **6** Tienes que tomar una manzanilla./ Debes tomar ... **7** Tienes que tomar un jarabe./ Debes tomar un ... **8** Tienes que ir al médico./ Debes ir al ...

5 **a** estantería **b** crema **c** resfriado **d** medicina **e** comprimidos

6 **a** Cosas positivas: Comer mucha fruta y verdura/ Beber mucha agua/ Usar aceite de oliva/ hacer ejercicio/ Dormir bastante   Cosas negativas: No comer muchas grasa ni dulces/ No beber mucho alcohol/ No fumar
   b Tienes que usar aceite de oliva./Debes usar .../Tienes que beber mucha agua./ Debes beber .../No tienes que beber mucho alcohol./ No debes beber .../No tienes que fumar./ No debes fumar .../Tienes que hace ejercicio./ Debes hacer ejercicio .../Tienes que dormir bastante./ Debes dormir bastante.

7 **1** es **2** Es **3** Es **4** está **5** Está **6** es **7** es **8** está **9** estás **10** estoy **11** estoy

UNIDAD 9

1 **Ir** al parque/ al cine/ de compras/ de copas/ a tomar unas copas **Hacer** la compra/ montañismo/ la cama **Jugar** al tenis/al fútbol

2 **a** Profesional soltera de 32 años, busca hombre serio y educado, entre 30 y 40 años. Me gusta jugar al tenis y correr. También me encantan los animales.

b Arquitecto divorciado de 40 años, sensible y culto, busca mujer sensible y divertida, entre 30 y 40 años. Me gusta el campo y viajar. ¡Ah! Me encantan los niños.

3 A Luisa le gusta Juan pero a Juan le gusta María pero .../A María le gusta Romeo pero a Romeo le gusta Marta .../Desafortunadamente a Marta le gusta Andrés pero a Andrés le gusta Luisa./¡Qué difícil!

4 El cumpleaños de la tía Clara es el tres de febrero./El cumpleaños del tío Pascual es el trece de julio./El cumpleaños de Rosi es el doce de diciembre./El santo de Rosi es el treinta uno de agosto./El cumpleaños de Ramón es el dos de noviembre./El santo de Ramón es el uno de mayo.

5 **a 1** ¿Tienen algo para comer? **2** ¿Algo más? **3** ¿Cuánto es? /¿Cuánto le debo? **4** ¿Qué van a tomar?
   b 1 d **2** c **3** b **4** a
   C A: ¿Qué van a tomar? B: Un café y un vino tinto. ¿Tienen algo para comer? A: Hay bocadillos de jamón, queso y tortilla. B: Uno de queso para mí. A: ¿Algo más? B: No, nada más. ¿Cuánto es? (¿Cuánto le debo?) A: Son 7.20 euros. B: Aquí tiene, gracias. A: A usted. Adiós.

6 *Cliente 1:* Para mí, una cerveza. *Cliente 2:* Yo (para mí) una café con leche. ¿Tienen bocadillos?/¿Qué tienen para comer? *Cliente 1:* Para mí, uno de queso. *Cliente 2:* Para mí, uno de jamón. (Five minutes later) *Cliente 1:* Para mí. El de jamón es para él./ para mi amigo. *Cliente 2:* ¿Cuánto es?/¿Cuánto le debo?

UNIDAD 10

1 **1** False **2** True **3** False **4** True **5** True **6** False **7** False

2 **1** en/ a **2** en **3** A: *de/ a* B: *en/(en: optional)* **4** a/ para **5** de/ para **6** without preposition **7** con/ en **8** con

3 **a** ¿A qué hora sale el tren? **b** ¿Puedo/Se puede pagar con tarjeta de crédito/con cheque? **c** ¿Puedo/Se puede fumar? **d** ¿Cómo puedo viajar? **e** ¿Qué prefieres, el tren o el coche? / ¿Qué transporte prefieres?

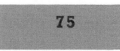

4 1 A: tienes B: Tengo ... 2 prefiere 3 A: prefiero B: preferimos 4 A: vuelve B: vuelve 5 B: duele A: te acuestas B: puedo/viene 6 empieza 7 quieres 8 podemos/empezamos

5 1 vienes 2 coger 3 dura 4 es 5 es 6 salen 7 puedo

6 *Querido/Querida ...*
¿Por qué no vienes a visitarme a Cáceres? Puedes coger el Talgo, un tren muy cómodo y rápido y en un momento estás aquí. El viaje sólo dura 2 horas y el billete no es muy caro, el billete de ida y vuelta sólo cuesta 21 €.
Los trenes salen todos los días a las 9 y a las 12 y yo puedo ir a recogerte a la estación.
Anímate y vente para Cáceres
Un abrazo

7 Buenos días, quería (quisiera/quiero) un billete de avión para Bilbao./Para el 28./¿Cuánto dura el viaje?/Entonces, quiero un billete para el vuelo de la una./Solo ida. ¿Qué precio tiene?/¿Cuánto cuesta?/Sí, con tarjeta de crédito./Es el ...

8 1 True 2 False 3 False 4 False

UNIDAD 11

1 a Quisiera (Quiero) reservar una habitación doble con cama de matrimonio./Para cinco noches./Del 18 al 22 de abril./Con baño./Your name./¿Cuánto es/ cuesta?/¿Está incluído el desayuno?

b Tengo reservada una habitación./Your name./¿A qué hora es el desayuno?/¿Hay una farmacia cerca de aquí?/(Muchas) gracias.

2 "Quisiera protestar por las malas condiciones de la habitación número 28. La ducha no funciona. El frigorífico tampoco funciona. No hay agua caliente. Tampoco hay papel higiénico ni jabón y las toallas están sucias."

3 1 piscina 2 aire acondicionado 3 calefacción 4 pista/cancha de tenis 5 peluquería 6 aparcamiento 7 cafetería 8 discoteca

4 *Londres, a 25 de mayo de 1995*
Muy Sres. míos:
Quisiera reservar una habitación doble, con dos camas para 16 noches, desde el 15 al 30 de junio. Quiero la habitación con baño completo. ¿Tienen las habitaciones aire acondicionado? También me gustaría saber si el hotel tiene piscina y pista de tenis.
Mi dirección es ... Mi teléfono:
En espera de sus noticias (su pronta respuesta).
Le saluda atentamente,

5 1 miércoles 2 siempre 3 ron 4 individual 5 salón 6 inglesa 7 tío 8 reservada 9 sucio CERVANTES

6 1 Parador de Aiguablava 2 Parador de Bielsa 3 Parador de Almagro 4 Parador de Bielsa 5 Parador de Almagro

7 a ¿Qué tipo de música es?/¿Dónde es?/¿Qué día es?/¿A qué hora es?/¿Cuánto cuesta la entrada?/¿Dónde está la Sala Universal?

UNIDAD 12

1 a **Ramiro:** México **Ester:** Cáceres **Ramón:** Tenerife

b **Tenerife:** 7 días/avión/ hotel con pensión completa/ 450 € **México:** 9 días/ avión y autobús/ hotel con desayuno/ 1280 € **Cáceres:** 5 días/ no incluye transporte/ incluye alojamiento pero no sabemos cuál/ 285 €

2 1 estuve 2 Llegué 3 me fui 4 tomé 5 visité 6 Subí 7 volví 8 tomé 9 comí 10 fui 11 pasé

3 ¿Qué película viste?/¿Te gustó?/¿Qué tal fue?/¿Dónde cenaste?/¿Qué tal?/¿Qué hiciste el domingo?

4 a el verano pasado/ayer/anoche/ anteayer/el mes pasado/la semana pasada/ en diciembre/el domingo

5 a Nos levantamos a las 9. Desayunamos en casa a las 9.30. A las 10.30 fuimos al mercado e hicimos la compra. A las doce/Al mediodía fuimos a un café a tomar algo. De una a cuatro estuvimos en el bingo. A las cuatro fuimos al cine y a las seis volvimos a casa. Cenamos a las ocho y desde las 9.30 hasta las once vimos la televisión. A las once nos acostamos.

b No fueron a una cafetería . Fueron a un bar y tomaron cerveza. A la una no fueron al bingo, comieron en un restaurante. No fueron al cine; vieron a un hombre sospechoso. No se acostaron a las once; salieron de casa y robaron el banco.

6 1 A 2 E 3 D 4 C 5 F 6 B

UNIDAD 13

1 Across: 1 natación 2 fútbol 3 equitación 4 voleibol **Down:** 1 baloncesto 2 golf 3 esquí 4 tenis 5 ciclismo 6 judo

2 Jugar: al tenis/ al fútbol/ al baloncesto/ al voleibol/ al golf **Montar:** a caballo/ en bicicleta **Hacer:** "footing"/ gimnasia/ judo **Practicar:** judo

4 a 9/ 1.30/ 3.00/ 4.30, 5.00/ 9.00
b A las 9 se levantaba, se tomaba un café con leche y se iba a la facultad. A la 1.30 volvía a su casa. A las 3.00 comía y descansaba. A las 4.30 o 5.00 volvía a la facultad. A las 9.00 volvía a casa, cenaba, leía, estudiaba, veía la televisión.

5 Cuando tenían 20 años Ana y Pedro eran pobres. Ahora son ricos./Antes trabajaban mucho y ahora trabajan poco./Vivían en un piso pequeño pero ahora viven en una casa con piscina./Antes comían en restaurantes baratos. Ahora comen en restaurantes caros./Cuando tenían 20 años no iban de vacaciones pero ahora van de vacaciones al extranjero a menudo./Antes no practicaban/ no hacían ningún deporte pero ahora hacen gimnasia y juegan al tenis./Cuando tenían 20 años tenían muchos amigos y ahora todavía tienen muchos amigos./Antes no tenían coche y ahora tienen dos coches.

UNIDAD 14

1 a 1 sol, despejado 2 cubierto, nublado 3 nevando 4 helada 5 viento 6 temperaturas altas 7 lloviendo 8 frío 9 nublado 10 neblina
b **Hace:** sol, viento, calor, frío **Hay:** helada, niebla, viento, neblina, temperaturas altas **Está:** lloviendo, nevando, despejado, nublado, cubierto
c cubierto, viento, heladas, despejado, sol, temperaturas, calor

2 soy/ estás/ hace/ está/ hizo/ estuvo/ hizo

3 **a** 1 Italia 2 Grecia 3 Alemania
4 Francia 5 Reino Unido/Gran Bretaña
6 Irlanda 7 España 8 Portugal

    b 1 En Italia hace calor pero está nublado
y lloviendo. 2 En Alemania hace sol con
temperaturas de 18 grados. 3 En el norte de
Francia está lloviendo. 4 En el sur de Francia
hace sol y hay tormentas. 5 En el Reino Unido
e Irlanda hace sol, pero en algunas partes está
lloviendo. 6 En el norte de la Península Ibérica
está lloviendo pero hace sol y calor en el centro.
7 Hay viento en la costa del sudoeste español.
8 En Grecia hace calor pero está nublado.

4 1 Pedro/ 40 años 2 Enrique/ 31 años
3 Luis/ 36 años 4 Juan/ 34 años

6 **a** 1 True 2 False 3 False

UNIDAD 15

1 **Pasar:** pasé, pasaste, pasó **Estudiar:**
estudié, estudiaste, estudió **Casarse:** me casé,
te casaste, se casó **Divorciarse:** me divorcié,
te divorciaste, se divorció **Nacer:** nací, naciste,
nació **Conocer:** conocí, conociste, conoció
Vivir: viví, viviste, vivió **Tener:** tuve, tuviste,
tuvo **Ir/Ser:** fui, fuiste, fue

2 **a/b** 1 True 2 True 3 True
4 True 5 True 6 False 7 False

    c 1 Lleva 35 años cantando. 2 Su
padre era ginecólogo. 3 Tuvo un accidente de
coche. 4 Se divorció en 1979.

3 Nació en Calzada de Calatrava en 1951.
Nueve años más tarde se trasladó a Madrigalejo
con su familia donde empezó sus estudios en el
Colegio de los Salesianos. En 1968 fue a Madrid
y empezó a trabajar en la Compañía Telefónica.
Entre 1977 y 1988 conoció a muchos artistas
importantes de la "Movida Madrileña". En
1980 terminó su trabajo en la Telefónica. En el
87 tuvo su primer éxito comercial y tres años
más tarde ganó el Premio Goya.

4 1 Llevo media hora esperando el autobús.
2 Hace diez años que vivo en Madrid.
3 Llevo tres meses estudiando español.
4 Hace siete años que hago natación. 5 Llevo
tres años jugando al fútbol. 6 Hace una
semana que leo este libro.

5 **a** 1 ¿En qué colegio estudiaste? 2
¿Cuánto tiempo viviste en Acapulco? 3
¿Dónde conociste a tu primer esposo? 4 ¿En
qué año os casasteis? 5 ¿Cuánto tiempo hace
que vives en La Habana? 6 ¿Haces gimnasia
con frecuencia/frecuentemente? 7 ¿Cuánto
tiempo llevas casada?

    b 1 estudió 2 vivió 3 conoció
4 se casaron 5 vive 6 hace 7 lleva

6 1 Mi marido y yo nos conocimos/nos
casamos/nos divorciamos en 1980. 2 Mi
amiga Lucía estuvo en Florida el año pasado.
3 No me gusta ir de compras. 4 Me levanto a
las ocho. 5 Ayer mis amigos y yo fuimos al
cine y vimos una película cubana que se llama
Fresas y Chocolate. 6 El poeta Ruben Darío
nació en 1867 y murió en 1916.

UNIDAD 16

1 1 b 2 h 3 f 4 a 5 g 6 c 7 e
8 d

2 ¿El restaurante (*name of the
restaurante*)?/Quisiera reservar una mesa./Del
Sr./ Srta./ Sra. *and your surname.*/Para el
sábado./Para dos./Para las nueve y
media./(Muchas) gracias./Adiós.

3 **Primero:** Espárragos con mayonesa/
Cóctel de gambas/ Espinacas a la catalana/ Sopa
de pescado **Segundo:** Chuletas de cerdo con
patatas/ Trucha a la navarra/ Huevos con
jamón/ Cordero asado **Postre:** Flan con nata/
Macedonia de frutas/ Helado/ Tarta de queso

4 **A:** ¿Qué van a tomar? **B:** Yo, de primero
sopa de ajo, y de segundo un filete a la plancha
con ensalada. **C:** Y, para mí, guisantes con
jamón y pollo al ajillo. **A:** ¿Y para beber?
B: Agua mineral con gas. **A:** ¿Qué van a
tomar de postre? **B:** Flan con nata y
macedonia de frutas.

5 1 Manolo es altísimo. 2 Ayer estuvimos
en un restaurante carísimo. 3 Las gambas
estaban riquísimas. 4 La conferencia fue
interesantísima. 5 Las espinacas están
buenísimas. 6 El domingo estuvimos en una
fiesta aburridísima. 7 El examen fue
dificilísimo.

6 1 True 2 True 3 False 4 True
5 False

UNIDAD 17

1 Barre el suelo/Lava la ropa/Haz la
comida/Limpia las ventanas/Plancha/Riega las
plantas/Haz la compra/Lleva a los niños al
parque/Ve a la farmacia y compra aspirinas/

2 1 Pase 2 Siéntese 2a duele
3 acuéstese 4 Levante 4a Le 5 Levántese
6 Tómese 6a póngase 7a Vuelva

3 Mira, sigue todo recto y toma la segunda calle
a la izquierda. Después sigue todo recto, cruza la
calle que te encuentras y sigue recto otra vez. Pasa
por debajo del puente y después gira a la derecha.
Continúa un poco y finalmente coge la primera a
la izquierda. Ese es el camino de casa. Tranquilo.

4 1 el poncho 2 la camisa 3 los
pantalones cortos 4 los pantalones 5 las
zapatillas de deporte (Sp)/ los zapatos de deporte
(LA) 6 el sombrero 7 los zapatos 8 la falda
9 la chaqueta (Sp)/ el saco (LA) 10 el vestido
11 la camiseta 12 las botas 13 la blusa

6 (Possible answers) 1 A Julia le gustaría
tener una casa más grande. 2 A Carla le
gustaría tocar mejor la trompeta. 3 A Andrés le
gustaría tener más vacaciones. 4 A Eva le
gustaría tener más tiempo libre/ más tiempo para
leer. 5 A Gabriel le gustaría tener un coche
nuevo. 6 A Angeles le gustaría trabajar menos/
tener menos trabajo.

7 1 True 2 False 3 True 4 False
5 False 6 True 7 True 8 True

9 (You have decided upon the importance of
each strategy. This order is just a suggestion. In
fact each strategy is very important.) 1 Deduce
el significado de palabras nuevas por el contexto
en el que están antes de mirar el significado. 2
Intenta no traducir literalmente. 3 Estudia un
poco cada día y revisa mucho. 4 Ten amigos
españoles y practica con ellos. 5 Escucha cintas.
6 Lee periódicos y libros. 7 Estudia gramática.
8 Haz ejercicios. 9 Escribe. 10 Haz listas o
diagramas con el vocabulario.

UNIDAD 18

1 **a** 1 B 2 F 3 A 4 C 5 D 6 E
7 G

    b 1 True 2 True 3 True 4 False.
Empieza a las 23.30. 5 False. Hay concierto
también el sábado y el domingo.

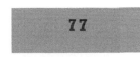

C 1 Ponen la película 'Hable con ella'.
2 Cierra a las 4 de la madrugada.
3 Un cantaor flamenco. **4** Las entradas cuestan entre 7 y 13 euros.

2 Hola, ¿está Rosa?/Bien. ¿Y tú?/¿Qué vais a hacer el viernes?/¿Queréis venir a X el sábado, entonces?/¿A qué hora?/¿Dónde nos vemos/ dónde quedamos?/Vale./ De acuerdo. Hasta el sábado.

3 a 1 malva **2** amarillo **3** rosa
4 zapato **5** oro
b marzo
C Ropa: vestido, chaqueta, calcetines, corbata, zapatos **Material:** lino, seda, lana, algodón, oro **Color:** malva, amarillo, verde, rojo, azul, gris **Dibujo:** rayas, lunares, cuadros, flores

4 1 unos zapatos marrones de piel/ unos zapatos de piel marrones **2** una camiseta de rayas roja y blanca de algodón **3** unos pantalones grises de algodón **4** una camisa de lino rosa **5** un jersey de lana rosa **6** unos calcetines blancos **7** una camisa de seda verde **8** unos pantalones cortos de algodón verdes

5 1 Quisiera probármelo. **2** ¿Puedo probármela? **3** Me los llevo. **4** ¿La tienen en otros colores? **5** Me las llevo. **6** ¿Puedo probármelos? **7** Me la llevo.

6 Buenos días. Quiero/ Quisiera unos pantalones negros./De la talla X o X./¿Los tienen en otros colores?/¿Puedo probarme los X?/¿Dónde están los probadores?/¿Me quedan bien?/¿Cuánto cuestan?/Vale, me los llevo.

7 1 La feria se celebra de 4 al 8 de diciembre. **2** Se celebra en Sevilla. **3** Participan doscientos productores/artesanos. **4** Cerámica, joyería, confección de tejidos, alfombras, piel ... **5** Los países son suramericanos: Bolivia, Perú, Argentina, Ecuador. **6** Representan a pequeñas empresas/ producción industrial a pequeña escala.

UNIDAD 19

1 Han visitado la Casa Rosada./Han comido en el restaurante Estancia./Van a ir a un espectáculo de tango./Han dado un paseo por el Parque Palermo./Han ido al Museo Histórico Nacional./Han visto a los amigos de Buenos

Aires./Van a comprar billete para Iguazú./Han reservado hotel en Puerto de Iguazú./Van a comprar recuerdos./Han hecho una excursión a Tigre./Van a hacer una excursión a Mar del Plata./Van a alquilar un coche.

2 1 ¿Has estado en la luna? **2** ¿Has subido al Himalaya? **3** ¿Has visto un ovni? **4** ¿Has comido pulpo? **5** ¿Has visto un fantasma? **6** ¿Has montado en camello? **7** ¿Te has emborrachado alguna vez? **8** ¿Te has enamorado alguna vez?

3 ya/ ya/ ya/ todavía no (or aún no)/ todavía (or aún)/ ya/ todavía (or aún)

4 1 Ya la he hecho./ Todavía no la he hecho. **2** Las he escuchado./ No las he escuchado. **3** Sí, lo he leído./ No, no lo he leído. **4** Ya los he terminado./ Todavía no los he terminado. **5** Sí, la he limpiado./ No, no la he limpiado. **6** Sí, los he visitado./ No los he visitado. **7** No, he ido en autobús./ Sí lo he tomado. **8** Sí, ya la he pagado./ Aún no la he pagado.

5 tenido/ pasado/ perdido/ llegado/ podido/ roto/ robado/ sido/ dado/ puesto/ ido

6 Nombre: Águeda/Robo/14/2/199../ C/ Fuencisla, al lado de los Almacenes Arias/Sí ha presentado denuncia./**Descripción de objeto y contenido:** era un bolso de piel marró. Llevaba 50 euros en metálico y todas las tarjetas de crédito. También tenía las llaves de casa y del coche,el permiso de conducir y una agenda roja.

7 Uno de los ladrones era alto y fuerte. Tenía las orejas grandes y el pelo corto. Era rubio y llevaba gafas de sol y barba. Llevaba una camiseta negra, unos pantalones tejanos, botas negras. En la mano llevaba una bolsa de plástico y una pistola. El otro era bajito y muy delgado. Tenía el pelo moreno y rizado. Tenía una nariz muy grande y llevaba bigote. Llevaba una cazadora vaquera, unos pantalones de jogging.

8 1 Latinoamérica es más importante que antes y la influencia de instituciones hispanas. **2** Falta de tradición y falta de profesores. **3** Mejores resultados en la comunicación al principio. **4** Entusiasmo de los profesores.

UNIDAD 20

1 1 puntual **2** recado **3** llamada **4** agenda **5** favor **6** pone **7** comunicando **8** equivocado TELEFONO

2 1 A: ¿Está Ana, por favor? **B:** ¿De parte de quién? **B:** No, no está. **A:** ¿Sabe cuándo volverá? **A:** Vale, dígale que me llame.
2 A: ¿Está Arturo? **B:** Sí, un momento ahora se pone. **A:** Hola Arturo, soy Paloma.
B: Hola Paloma, ¿qué tal? **A:** Muy bien. ¿Y tú? **B:** Estoy muy cansado. Tengo muchísimo trabajo. **A:** ¿Quieres venir a cenar a mi casa mañana por la noche? **C:** Lo siento, pero es que tengo que terminar un informe para el lunes. **A:** Adiós. **3 A:** Seat, ¿Dígame? **B:** ¿Puede ponerme con la Srta. Balduque? **A:** ¿De parte de quién? **B:** De la Srta. López, de Fiat. **A:** Un momento, ahora le paso. **A:** Lo siento, la Srta. Balduque está en una reunión. ¿Quiere dejarle un recado? **B:** Sí, dígale que he llamado y que volveré a llamar más tarde.

3 A: ¿Qué podemos hacer el domingo? **B:** Me gustaría ir a una exposición. **A:** Muy bien, hay una muy interesante en el Retiro. **B:** ¿Quedamos a las 12.00? **A:** No, prefiero más tarde. ¿Te va bien a la una? **B:** De acuerdo, entonces quedamos a la una. **A:** ¿Dónde quedamos? **B:** Podemos quedar en la Puerta de Alcalá. **A:** Vale, nos vemos a la una en la Puerta de Alcalá.

4 a Buenos días./¿Me pone con la Srta. Puig del departamento de Ventas?/De X de Resaca Radio en Londres./Hola Elena, soy X de Radio Candela./Bien ¿y tú?/Iré/ Voy a ir a Barcelona la próxima semana y me gustaría/ quisiera concertar una cita para hablar de los nuevos productos./Sí, ¿a qué hora?/Mejor a las 10. ¿Dónde nos vemos/ quedamos?/Vale, te enviaré un fax, confirmando todos los detalles./ Hasta pronto./ Adiós.
b From: Resaca Radio, London
To: Elena Puig. Radio Candela
Departamento de Ventas.

Llegaré el día 31 de mayo a las 7.30. Estaré en el Hotel Continental, habitación 231. El teléfono es el 4 159293. Te veré en tu oficina, el jueves día 1 a las 10.
Saludos,

5 1 Cáncer **2** Aries **3** Sagitario
4 Virgo **5** Libra